Social Movements and Transformation

Series Editor
Berch Berberoglu, Sociology, University of Nevada, Reno, USA

This series tackles one of the central issues of our time: the rise of large-scale social movements and the transformation of society over the last thirty years. As global capitalism continues to affect broader segments of the world's population workers, peasants, the self-employed, the unemployed, the poor, indigenous peoples, women, and minority ethnic groups there is a growing mass movement by the affected populations to address the inequities engendered by the globalization process. These popular mass movements across the globe (such as labor, civil rights, women's, environmental, indigenous, and anti-corporate globalization movements) have come to form a viable and decisive force to address the consequences of the operations of the transnational corporations and the global capitalist system. The study of these social movements their nature, social base, ideology, and strategy and tactics of mass struggle is of paramount importance if we are to understand the nature of the forces that are struggling to bring about change in the global economy, polity, and social structure. This series aims to explore emerging movements and develop viable explanations for the kind of social transformations that are yet to come.

Matt Reichel

Teacher Power in the Digital Age

The Fight for the Soul of American Public Education in the Early 21st Century

Matt Reichel
Journalism and Digital Communication
University of South Florida
St. Petersburg, USA

ISSN 2946-2193   ISSN 2946-2207 (electronic)
Social Movements and Transformation
ISBN 978-3-031-87190-0   ISBN 978-3-031-87191-7 (eBook)
https://doi.org/10.1007/978-3-031-87191-7

© The Author(s), under exclusive license to Springer Nature Switzerland AG 2025

This work is subject to copyright. All rights are solely and exclusively licensed by the Publisher, whether the whole or part of the material is concerned, specifically the rights of translation, reprinting, reuse of illustrations, recitation, broadcasting, reproduction on microfilms or in any other physical way, and transmission or information storage and retrieval, electronic adaptation, computer software, or by similar or dissimilar methodology now known or hereafter developed.
The use of general descriptive names, registered names, trademarks, service marks, etc. in this publication does not imply, even in the absence of a specific statement, that such names are exempt from the relevant protective laws and regulations and therefore free for general use.
The publisher, the authors and the editors are safe to assume that the advice and information in this book are believed to be true and accurate at the date of publication. Neither the publisher nor the authors or the editors give a warranty, expressed or implied, with respect to the material contained herein or for any errors or omissions that may have been made. The publisher remains neutral with regard to jurisdictional claims in published maps and institutional affiliations.

Cover illustration: Antons Jevterevs/Alamy Stock Photo

This Palgrave Macmillan imprint is published by the registered company Springer Nature Switzerland AG
The registered company address is: Gewerbestrasse 11, 6330 Cham, Switzerland

If disposing of this product, please recycle the paper.

Competing Interests The author has no competing interests to declare that are relevant to the content of this manuscript.

Contents

1 Teachers in the Streets — 1
   The Book's Organization and Central Arguments — 12
   References — 14

2 Teachers in the Digital Imaginary — 17
   The Roots of the Digital Activist Imaginary — 19
   A Hybrid Movement — 25
   Teachers and the Digital Citizenry — 27
   Social Movement Unionism — 29
   Facebook and a New Repertoire of Contention — 36
   References — 39

3 Teachers in the Material Reality — 41
   Central Assumptions of a Cyclical Analysis of History — 42
   The Crisis of Fordism and Birth of Neoliberalism — 44
   The Birth of Neoliberal Education Reforms — 46
      From Monitoring to Control — 49
   References — 52

4 Teachers in the Broader Struggles Over Class, Race, and Gender — 55
   Teachers as a Contradictory Class — 57
   The Origin of Capitalist Patriarchy — 59
   Professional Autonomy and its Contradictions — 62
   Race and Racism in the Battle for the Soul of Education — 66

	Struggles Both Old and New	68
	References	69
5	**Teachers in the Circuits of Communication**	71
	Education and the Interdiscursive Struggle Over Policy Frames	75
	Mass Media's Role: Naturalizing the Crisis Trope	78
	A Heuristic Model of Discursive Flows on Education	81
	On the Relationship Between Structure and Practice	88
	From the "Crisis of Education" to the "Battle for the Soul of Education"	90
	A Discursive Struggle	92
	References	93
6	**Teachers in the Networks of Crowd Mobilization**	97
	Identifying Purpose in Social Media Practice	98
	A Heuristic of Social Media Purpose	101
	Narration of Cause	103
	Mobilization	106
	Motivation	109
	Discussion/Information	115
	A Communicative Cycle of Contention	117
	References	118
7	**Teachers in the Dominant News Discourses**	119
	Identifying Frames in the Dominant News Coverage	121
	A Shift to the Left Bounds of the Neoliberal Paradigm	125
	Finally Some Discussion of Issues	134
	References	136
8	**Conclusion: Teacher Activism in Reactionary Times**	139
	References	147

References 149

Index 157

List of Figures

Fig. 5.1 Interdiscursive cycle of education and practice 82
Fig. 6.1 Distribution of posts by category of purpose in state level Facebook groups during 2018 uprising 102

List of Tables

Table 7.1 Distribution of Framing Categories in Articles Inspected During the 2012 CTU Strike   125
Table 7.2 Distribution of Framing Categories in Articles Inspected During the 2018 Strike Wave   126

CHAPTER 1

Teachers in the Streets

Abstract This chapter begins with a vignette about teachers in Kentucky organizing during the broader national movement in the spring of 2018. The uprising in that state was provoked by then-governor Matt Bevin's attempt to force through teacher pension reforms as part of a sewerage bill at the 11th hour of a legislative session. As teacher activists began mobilizing against the reforms, organizing several walkouts and marches on the state capitol, the governor scolded them for having the temerity to cancel classes, declaring: "I guarantee you somewhere in Kentucky today a child was sexually assaulted that was left at home because there was nobody there to watch them." Outrage over these remarks spurred thousands more into the streets in subsequent rallies. I then introduce the following core arguments of the book. Firstly, by organizing a broader public of affected parties, including parents and community members around schools—both online and offline—I contend that the teachers' movement has marked the beginnings of a broader sectoral shift toward social movement unionism, particularly in Chicago, where the militant CORE slate has now presided over the CTU for a decade. Secondly, as a result of this shift in organization, I argue that the teachers' movement constitutes a discursive and pedagogical intervention against the metric-driven neoliberal logics that have been effectively codified into law via successive reforms promulgated at all levels of government. Thirdly, by engaging with critical theorists in the domain of media and cultural studies, this book offers a framework for understanding the interplay

© The Author(s), under exclusive license to Springer Nature
Switzerland AG 2025
M. Reichel, *Teacher Power in the Digital Age*, Social Movements and Transformation, https://doi.org/10.1007/978-3-031-87191-7_1

between education and other cultural institutions in the constitution of the prevailing hegemonic consensus.

Keywords Chicago Teachers' Union · Caucus of Rank-and-File organizing · 2018 teacher strikes · 2018 teacher uprising · Social movement unionism

Kevin Presnell, a high school civics teacher at Madison Central High School in Richmond, Kentucky, and local building rep for Kentucky Education Association (KEA), echoed a sentiment that I heard numerous times in my preliminary discussions with teachers involved in the uprising in the state earlier this year. That is, despite his involvement with the KEA, he never considered himself an activist prior to this. He identifies as a Republican, and lives in one of the reddest parts of a state that has sided with the Republican presidential nominee in eight of the last 10 elections.

However, a veritable fuse was lit as the state legislature debated an overhaul of teacher's pensions. The changes would have limited the number of sick days that could be exchanged, while placing new hires in a hybrid system wherein eventual payouts would be unknown prior to the time of retirement. As activist teachers began clamoring against the reforms, organizing several walkouts and marches on the state capitol, Governor Matt Bevin scolded them for having the temerity to cancel classes, declaring: "I guarantee you somewhere in Kentucky today a child was sexually assaulted that was left at home because there was nobody there to watch them" (McLaren & Aulbach, 2018).

These remarks spurred thousands more out into the streets in subsequent rallies. Even those who never previously identified as a political activist joined the fray, as the movement was less rooted in issues bridging traditional political fault lines, and more about defending the integrity of their profession from attacks by political leaders. Presnell notes: "This movement was instigated by the governor, and emboldened by West Virginia," referring to the wildcat strike in the state bordering Kentucky to the east.

Moreover, the legislative chicanery around the pension reforms, introduced at the 11th hour in a sewerage bill, felt particularly dehumanizing to a workforce that has already endured decades of austerity. Many took this gambit as symbolic of how teaching had been devalued as a profession. Maggie Roll, a ninth-year Spanish high school teacher in Hazard, KY, pondered: "How will we recruit the best teachers when we are on the same level as the sewerage?" This feeling of disrespect that Roll describes has been the principal driving force of the teacher uprising over the last decade, which hit its crescendo in 2018, when thousands of teachers in jurisdictions throughout the country took part in myriad protest actions, including wildcat strikes, walkouts, sickouts, and massive marches and rallies.

This rolling wave of teacher actions commenced in West Virginia, where frustration with stagnant wages and rising health care costs led teachers and other education personnel to strike across all 55 of the state's counties beginning on February 22, a day after the Republican governor, Jim Justice, signed a bill that would have given teachers a 2% raise that year, with an additional 1% raise each of the subsequent years. Movement leaders argued that this was not enough to keep up with inflation, especially in a state that ranked 48th in terms of teacher pay. The strike continued until March 7, after the state legislature approved a 5% pay increase for teachers, though the issue of health care costs remained unresolved.

In short order, teachers in other states followed suit, including neighboring Kentucky, as well as Oklahoma, Arizona, North Carolina, and Colorado. Smaller actions were taken at the local level in a number of other places, including Los Angeles, Atlanta, and Oakland. Teachers in Chicago, who took part in a weeks-long labor stoppage in 2012, went on strike again in 2019. The issues raised varied by locale and included teacher pay and pensions, education funding, school conditions, class sizes, how education is funded, and the use of alternative "choice" schools such as voucher and charter schools. In most of these states, teachers connected their grievances to broader social issues. For example, West Virginia teachers rallied alongside other public sector workers, while teachers in Oklahoma organized parents and other community members concerned about inadequate education funding. Meanwhile, the Chicago Teachers' Union's (CTU) ruling slate—the Caucus of Rank-and-File Educators (CORE)—has pioneered broader community engagement as an organizing tactic since the slate's inception.

Because of its significant contributions to the struggle of teachers and their various allies in the communities around the public schools they represent, the CTU has been instrumental to the story of heightened teacher militancy in recent years. No organizing body has played as integral a role in the fight for education justice since the ruling CORE slate assumed leadership of the union in 2010. In addition to their groundbreaking work in building community ties, they have also introduced a bottom-up approach to organizing that emphasizes the work of local school liaisons. Moreover, they have expanded the range of issues raised to include criticisms of various facets of the neoliberal reform agenda, most notably the shuttering of traditional public schools in favor of charter schools.

While state law forbids negotiation on non-contractual issues during the collective bargaining process, the CTU has used community organizing and social media as vehicles to raise these issues in the public consciousness while framing their activism as being in the interest of the broader public. Their argument is that shuttering a local public school does not just adversely impact the teachers working at the school, but the entire neighborhood that relied on that school to educate their kids and to serve as a resource and gathering place.

Not only has CORE introduced all of these important innovations, but they have had tremendous success in doing so. They have led teachers out on two successful strikes—in 2012 and 2019—during which they mobilized the broader public around issues of education justice. The union has also gotten involved in the electoral arena, playing an integral role in the election of several progressive and socialist city council members, in addition to the newly elected mayor, Brandon Johnson, who was a CTU organizer during the 2012 strike before launching his political career.

Nonetheless, the central focus of this book is not on retelling the history of the CTU's reform efforts or the various teacher strikes and walkouts that have occurred in recent years. There is already plenty of literature available recounting these histories, including Uetricht and Ashby and Bruno's insightful work on the CTU strike, as well as Eric Blanc's book on the 2018 rolling uprising. There is other excellent scholarship looking at the organizing tactics of the CTU and other "social movement unions," including Jane McAlevey's *No Shortcuts*. This book does not seek to replicate any of this indispensable work, though I will draw from them in framing the story of recent teacher activism as part of the ongoing rupture of the neoliberal governing consensus. In so doing, I focus on some broader questions. Why is all of this teacher activism happening now and how does it fit into the larger cycle of contestation ongoing over the last 30 years? How do educational institutions reflect broader social crises and struggles? And what does this tell us about the relationship between education and society as a whole?

In other words, this book is not just about teachers' unions and their organizational activities. It is about how teacher activists—often working outside of their formal union channels—fit into the larger story of digitally enabled activism. I situate the teachers' movement of the last two decades among the broader wave of movements that have occurred throughout the world during this time, including the *Arab Spring* protests in Tunisia and Egypt, the *Indignados* in Spain, as well as the *Occupy* movement and *Black Lives Matter* in the United States. I adopt Gerbaudo's (2012) terminology—"movements of the squares"—in categorizing this wave of contestation, as the congregation in highly visible public demonstrations has been so important to all of these movements: what he describes as the "*material precipitation* from symbolic assemblages to bodily assemblages in public space" (p. 42).

In this formulation, activists initially connect around common grievances on social media before pivoting to congregation in a specific place that ultimately becomes the physical embodiment of the movement. For the occupy movement, that meant encampments at Zuccotti Park (near Wall Street) in New York as well as other centrally located public parks in cities and towns throughout the country. In the case of Arab Spring activists in Egypt, the assembly occurred in Tahrir Square in Cairo. For activist teachers, the material precipitation has occurred in state legislative houses and on picket lines in front of schools and district buildings. In all cases, the public manifestations became a rallying point for activists and outside supporters.

Like Gerbaudo (2012), I contend that these movements are all born of the ongoing crisis of neoliberal hegemony. This book takes it as a given that neoliberalism—as a set of principles seeking to use government to best harness market logics, often to the detriment of public and social infrastructure, including public education—has come into a crisis of reproduction. Over much of the last decade, the signs of crisis are abundant: not only in the emergence of these movements amid the heightened precariousness and alienation of large parts of the working population, but also in the weakening of the political center line and the rise of once dormant tendencies on both the left and right, from the socialism of Bernie Sanders, Alexandria Ocasio-Cortez, and Jeremy Corbyn to the neo-nationalist reaction of Donald Trump, Boris Johnson, and Narendra

Modi. At the same time, public mistrust of political and media institutions—two key pillars of any democratic system—has steadily risen over the last few decades, particularly on the extreme right.

In order to build upon this fundamental argument that neoliberalism is in crisis, it is worth stopping to define the term as it applies to this book. To that end, I turn to Pauline Lipman (2011) who provides trenchant analysis of how neoliberal reforms were enacted in Chicago's housing, development, and education policy over the final decades of the twentieth century and first decades of the twenty-first century. She says:

> Neoliberalism is an ensemble of economic and social policies, forms of governance, and discourses and ideologies that promote individual self-interest, unrestricted flows of capital, deep reductions in the cost of labor, and sharp retrenchment of the public sphere. Neoliberals champion privatization of social goods and withdrawal of government from provision for social welfare on the premise that competitive markets are more effective and efficient. Neoliberalism is not just "out there" as a set of policies and explicit ideologies. It has developed as a new social imaginary, a common sense about how we think about society and our place in it. (6)

For the purposes of this book, it is important to have this understanding of neoliberalism as both a set of specific policy prescriptions and a social imaginary that legitimates those policies. These are the two fronts that teacher activists have had to fight at once. On the one hand, neoliberal education policy has sought to undermine traditional public schools by underfunding them and diverting resources to alternatives like charter schools and voucher programs, and, on the other hand, neoliberal ideologues have promulgated a social imaginary that depicts anything public as inherently wasteful, dysfunctional, and inefficient. Public schools have been particularly singled out for derision as a place where inept, lazy teachers allow wayward and undisciplined students to run amok (as evinced in dominant pop culture tropes detailed in Chapter 5). In this rendering, school administrators and teachers must be brought into line with a healthy dose of market discipline.

Neoliberal education reforms have focused on the five following areas: tightening public education budgets with a particular focus on subjects deemed non-essential, such as the arts and foreign languages; increasing the number of standardized tests and other forms of state-mandated curricula; tying education funding and teaching promotions more narrowly to the results of standardized tests; and closing schools deemed "failing" by standardized test metrics and privileging so-called "choice schools," such as charter and voucher schools in their stead, because these schools more closely align with the market logics privileged by the overarching reform process (Goldstein, D., 2014; Lipman, 2011).

For teachers, this has translated into losing some of the autonomy they had gained in previous struggles. There is less space for teachers to experiment with different pedagogical methods and to tailor course modalities to their specific skill set when there is such intense pressure surrounding test results. In many states, the curriculum is now set at the state or district level, so teachers are reduced to classroom managers more so than pedagogical professionals. At the same time, teaching positions are generally less stable than they were prior to the era of neoliberal reforms, thus contributing to an overarching sense of stress in the workplace.

Meanwhile, reformers have effectively driven a wedge between teachers and the public that they serve. As elaborated in Chapter 3, the neoliberal education reform process began with a conscious effort by the Reagan administration to sow distrust of teachers in the eyes of the public. The education czar at the time, Terrel Bell, commissioned the publication of *A Nation at Risk*, an alarmist report about the purported crisis in America's schools, with blame narrowly placed on a teacher corps that was portrayed as uniquely unqualified. The policy that was subsequently put into place throughout the country has, in turn, tended to hold teachers solely responsible for standardized test results that typically reflect broader socioeconomic realities more so than the effectiveness of any individual instructor.

Teacher activists, especially in militant reformist unions like the CTU, have sought to rebuild the trust of their communities by organizing alongside them. Rather than viewing education issues as narrowly impacting the livelihood of teachers, they have framed these issues as touching the entire communities that are affected by the closure of local public schools. When a local public school is closed, the community loses a valuable resource that not only educates its children, but also cares for them, provides counseling services, and serves as a cultural nexus for students and the broader community alike.

The teachers' movement seeks to reclaim education as a public good in much the same way that the other "movements of the squares" have sought to reclaim public space that has been lost to neoliberalism's quest to privatize and monetize public resources. During the Arab

Spring, activists in Turkey gathered in a public square—Gezi Park—that authorities had slated for private development. Likewise, *Occupy* activists erected encampments near Wall Street and other highly visible public places to express a symbolic sentiment about the conquest of the public by private interests. As many scholars and commentators have noted, the lines between private and public have been blurred by neoliberal logics privileging financial flows over notions of collective good, and these movements have sought to reassert those borders.

Meanwhile, it is important to stress that the impacts of neoliberalism have not just been confined to a few localities. It has been the dominant—that is, hegemonic—ideology of the global capitalist system for roughly half a century now. However, it is facing a crisis of reproduction that has created a rupture along which the major political fault lines now fall. And this is why the major movements of the era have tended to pose themselves against neoliberal policies in their various manifestations. Animating this political struggle is a discursive tension between the rationalization of market logics intrinsic to neoliberalism, on the one hand, and an amorphous "other" seeking to recenter some notion of the collective in the political imaginary on the other hand. This popular embrace of an alternative to neoliberalism, whatever its form, serves as the backbone of the digital activist imaginary discussed in the next chapter. The development of digital media technologies has opened new pathways for political discourse that has, in turn, given rise to expressions of frustration with the prevailing system of neoliberal governance and a desire for governance that is more responsive to public needs.

I argue that the teachers' movement presents a privileged vantage point from which to glimpse this discursive tension, owing to the centrality of educational institutions in the broader cultural arena, and the specific focus placed on education policy by neoliberal reformers. In illuminating the discourses around education policy and practice over the last 50 years, this book addresses a number of interrelated questions: how is this movement similar to other movements of the era, most notably the "movements of the squares" that have emerged out of the resentment of increasingly precarious populations in countries throughout the world? Why has the teachers' movement become so integral to the contestation of neoliberalism in its moment of crisis? What does this say, more broadly, about the importance of teachers and education in the ongoing struggle? What are the dominant discourses in both the mass media and political terrain about education and teachers, generally, and the teachers' movement, in particular, and how do these reflect governing neoliberal logics? How do these discourses differ from the way that teachers themselves talk about their work, both in interviews and in their organizing on social media? How has this discursive tension illuminated the crisis of social reproduction facing neoliberal capitalism and the broader social crisis? What does this political struggle around education tell us about the role of education in constituting and reshaping the prevailing hegemonic consensus?

To develop this analysis, I draw on scholarship connecting the neoliberal ideological project to the education reforms that animate the current struggle (Apple, 2001, 2006, 2013; Berliner & Biddle, 1995; Lipman, 2011), as well as literature on news media framing as both justifying and naturalizing the reforms comporting with the neoliberal counteroffensive of this era and use this literature to inform the empirical analysis of news reportage of the movement (Apple 2001, 2013; Berliner & Biddle, 1995; Goldstein, D., 2014; Goldstein, R., 2011; Lipman, 2011). This project connects these strands by showing how educational discourses and dominant pedagogies have served to help legitimate the prevailing hegemonic order, while producing the contradictions that are now animating its crisis of reproduction.

As a result, this book is also not just about how teacher activists fit into the dominant wave of contestation of the last 15 years. It is, by necessity, about something more fundamental: how teachers and the schools that they work in, as a whole, fit into the society that they operate in. The more I pursued this project, the more I came to realize that when one talks about education policy and teachers' unions issues, one inevitably gets into larger questions about how schools relate to the communities they serve.

After all, education is not just a site where pupils learn and teachers work. It is much more than that. It is where young people learn to socialize with others and come to understand the diversity of viewpoints that exist in society. In the Deweyan view of things, it is where they learn to address social problems and develop the critical thinking skills necessary to be a functioning member of a democratic polity. Schools are also a gathering site for community organizations, including parent–teacher associations, local school councils, and other local clubs and associations.

In other words, education is a core cultural institution: one that reflects all of the different aspects to the society that contains it, including its different peoples, ideas, values, and all of the tensions and contradictions that undergird these things. In that respect, education is an incubator in which society is reproduced and in which the dominant paradigm of any given society can be contested and transformed (Apple 1995, 2001, 2013; Bowles & Gintis, 1976). In the Gramscian formulation, it is a central site in the formulation and contestation of the prevailing hegemonic consensus (Gramsci, 1971). And this is why education has been the focal point of neoliberal reformers for half a century and, in turn, has become such a central flashpoint for the ongoing political tensions marking neoliberalism's ongoing crisis of reproduction.

It is also worth noting that teacher activists do not envision themselves as *just* workers fighting for better wages. They tend to see their movement as being about something bigger, epitomized by a famous remark of former CTU president Karen Lewis, who described her union's 2012 strike as being about "the very soul of public education, not only in Chicago but everywhere." The CTU has raised myriad issues in their various campaigns, including opposition to closures of traditional public schools in favor of charter schools, advocating for improvement to the material infrastructure of the schools, and opposition to the mandate that teacher performance be tied to the results of standardized test scores. The CTU recognized that their battles are the same ones going on nationally, and thus framed their movement as one designed to inspire similar actions elsewhere: a nation-wide struggle over the purpose of education in society.

Of course, there have long been political battles over all aspects to education policy, including curriculum, methods of instruction, course content, and how students and teachers should be evaluated. However, the nature of the current struggle is unique in that so much of the focus is on fundamental pedagogical questions about how to evaluate students, teachers, schools, and entire school systems.

My contention is that the teacher movement constitutes a counterhegemonic pedagogy challenging the neoliberal paradigm in its educational manifestation. While the neoliberal view of education is narrowly focused on the cultivation of good workers for capital, the counterhegemonic of pedagogical practice views education as a public good in which schools perform a vital public service: that of serving as an important anchor in the communities they are embedded in, while cultivating the engaged citizenry necessary for a robust democracy. The neoliberal pedagogy sees low-scoring schools on standardized tests as expendable, while activist teachers embracing a counterhegemonic pedagogy see schools as vital anchors of the community. The prevailing metric-driven approach to education policy has been determined for decades now at the federal level by *No Child Left Behind* and *Race to the Top*, the education policy laws passed under the second Bush and Obama administrations, respectively, which have tied federal education dollars to standardized test results, resulting in the shuttering of schools deemed "failing" by these scores. As a result, activist teachers, especially in Chicago, have organized larger social movements incorporating community groups impacted by school closures (Brogan, 2014; Lipman, 2011).

The neoliberal pedagogy sees students and teachers as data points, while the counterhegemonic view sees both as vital members of the community that they inhabit. This tension mirrors the dichotomy elaborated by Paulo Freire (1970/2018) between the banking concept of education and the dialogical approach to instruction. The former views knowledge as something that is deposited into people from above, which concretizes a hierarchical view of the world where superiors are the distributors of worthwhile knowledge to pupils. The dialogical approach, meanwhile, emphasizes problem-solving as the goal of education and encourages pupils to arrive at solutions on their own through the investigation of generative themes. This encouragement of student thinking and problem-solving, in turn, creates a sense of empowerment in students, as education ceases to be an abstract exercise, and, instead, is connected to their own lived reality.

This core tension between knowledge as a commodity and knowledge as an instrument of critical thinking and problem-solving has always existed. Individual schools and districts have long faced internal battles on questions of pedagogical practice turning on these fundamental questions of what approach serves students best. What is different in the contemporary United States is that official policy prescriptions have had such sway on the realities of individual districts and schools through reforms passed at all levels, including *No Child Left Behind* and *Race to the Top*, which have forcefully steered instruction in the direction of the banking model of pedagogical practice.

Given that these policies of pedagogical control have come during an era of substantial decline in union membership and power, while wages and benefits have stagnated, teachers have faced unique pressures to conform to the mandates handed down to them by policymakers. They are in an increasingly precarious economic position at the same time that outside forces have taken ever greater control of education policy. In short, the current education climate is one defined by a power imbalance between elite reformers and educators that have been increasingly marginalized by the neoliberal policy, thus heightening the tension between the two imaginaries that animate each sector of society: a neoliberal imaginary that seeks to control its subjects and an alternative "other" that seeks to recapture ground lost during the period of neoliberal retrenchment.

The Book's Organization and Central Arguments

In highlighting this struggle over educational policy and addressing the questions enumerated above, I start by delving into greater detail about recent teacher uprisings and the broader wave of protest into which I situate this movement in Chapter 2. I elaborate more on the radical digital imaginary that has animated these movements and discuss some of the ways that other scholars have attempted to make sense of the contentious subject that has emerged out of these movements.

I then highlight the material realities facing teachers and other activists as neoliberalism has come into a crisis of reproduction in Chapter 3. I delineate the history of education reforms promulgated in the early years of neoliberal retrenchment and the political rhetoric employed to justify those reforms. This history starts with the Reagan administration's rhetoric about a "crisis in education," which tended to place disproportionate and undue blame on teachers for failures that were largely out of their control. I situate these reforms within broader historical systems of class and gender-based subjugation in Chapter 4, especially focusing on how education has long been singled out as an arena for disciplinary reform because of the highly gendered nature of its workforce.

In Chapter 5, I engage with critical theory in cultural studies and education to address questions around the role of education in the cultivation of the dominant subjects of any given era of capitalist production. I build on this existing theory by offering a model to chart the flow of discourses across societal circuits: from education to the political arena to the broader society. I then highlight how these political discourses have transferred to dominant news media coverage in Chapter 6, which includes a frame analysis of hundreds of news articles in major national news publications covering both the 2012 CTU strike and the 2018 uprising.

This book also incorporates the results of dozens of semi-structured interviews with teacher activists involved in the 2018 rolling strike wave, as well as a content analysis of thousands of Facebook posts by teachers involved in the same uprising. The interviews are incorporated throughout the book, but they are especially prevalent as the history of recent teacher organizing is fleshed out in Chapters 2 and 3. The content analysis of Facebook posts is discussed in Chapter 7 as part of a discussion of social media organizing tactics.

In telling this history and synthesizing the results of these empirical studies, my discussion is guided by the following core arguments:

1. Firstly, I contend that the teachers' movement is best situated among the broader "movements of the squares" wave of protest—including the Occupy movement, Black Lives Matter, and the Arab Spring. I argue that these movements, in turn, have their origin in the Global Social Justice Movement of the late 1990s and early 2000s, These movements all share a common radical imaginary in opposition to the global neoliberal consensus, which they see as having captured major political, economic, and cultural institutions in societies throughout the world.
2. The teachers' movement is unique in this wave of contestation in that it has taken on a hybrid form—combining the digitally enabled communicative tactics of contemporary movements with the institutionally grounded union politics of older movements. It shares much in common with the uprisings of "digital citizens," but it does not embrace the prefigurative politics of radical horizontality that has animated those movements, thus sparing it the problem of ephemerality that has plagued other movements in this wave of contestation.
3. This hybrid activism has involved interrelated organizational and communicative interventions on the part of teachers through which they have incorporated broader publics into their organizing efforts, as part of an effort to contest the hegemonic neoliberal ideology as it manifests in official education policy and the broader discourses that legitimate it.
4. In engaging with a broader public of affected parties, including parents and community members around schools—both online and offline—the teachers' movement has marked the beginnings of a sectoral shift toward social movement unionism, particularly in Chicago, where the militant CORE slate has now led the CTU for over a decade.

5. In this regard, much of the ongoing struggle is about how society conceives of the role of education in society. I contend that neoliberal reforms have served to heighten the tension between a "public service" view of education versus one that sees education as an economic instrumentality. The discursive intervention of teacher activists is to, effectively, push the prevailing discourse in the direction of the former.
6. Because of the centrality of education as a cultural arena, I argue that teacher activists are also impacting larger political fault lines. In fleshing out this argument, I engage with critical scholarship in both the cultural studies and education areas to advance theory about the flow of discourses and logics between educational institutions and the broader society that contains them.

Teacher activists derive power from their capacity to shift the discursive needle while also being materially grounded via their connection to a core cultural institution. As a result, they can engage the radical imaginary of other movements, while connecting with the broader communities that their schools serve. Schools are incubators for the rest of society, reflecting dominant paradigms and the struggles that undergird them. As such, the story of what goes on in schools is also necessarily a story about what has gone on in the societies that contain them. In this case, that narrative is about the implementation of the neoliberal project within the cultural apparatus and the resentment that the associated reforms have sparked among workers and concerned community members across the country. In short, it is about the struggle of neoliberal reformers to realize their vision in the face of an activist imaginary that has blossomed in the early decades of the digital age.

References

Apple, M. (1995). *Education and power* (2nd ed.). Routledge.
Apple, M. (2001). *Educating the right way: Markets, standards, god, and inequality*. Routledge.
Apple, M. (2006). *Educating the right way*. Routledge.
Apple, M. (2013). *Can education change society?* Routledge.
Berliner, D., & Biddle, B. (1995). *The Manufactured crisis: Myths, fraud and the attack on America's public schools*. Addison-Wesley.

Bowles, S., & Gintis, H. (1976). *Schooling in capitalist America: Educational reform and the contradictions of economic life*. Basic Books.
Brogan, P. (2014). Getting to the CORE of the Chicago Teachers' Union transformation. *Studies in Social Justice, 8*(2), 145–164.
Freire, P. (2018). *Pedagogy of the oppressed*. Bloomsbury Publishing (Original work published 1970).
Gerbaudo, P. (2012). *Tweets and the streets: Social media and contemporary activism*. London: Pluto Press.
Goldstein, D. (2014). *The teacher wars: A history of America's most embattled profession*. Doubleday.
Goldstein, R. (2011). Imaging the frame: Media representations of teachers, their unions, NCLB, and education reform. *Educational Policy, 25*(4), 543–576.
Gramsci, A. (1971). In Q. Hoare, & G. Nowell-Smith (Eds.), *Selections from the prison notebooks of Antonio Gramsci*. International Publishers.
Lipman, P. (2011). *The new political economy of urban education: Neoliberalism, race, and the right to the city*. Routledge.
McLaren, M., & Aulbach, L. (2018, April 13). Bevin: Children were sexually assaulted and tried drugs because teachers were protesting. *Louisville Courier-Journal*. https://www.courier-journal.com/story/news/politics/ky-legislature/2018/04/13/matt-bevin-kentucky-governor-children-sexually-assaulted-teacher-protests/516569002/

CHAPTER 2

Teachers in the Digital Imaginary

Abstract This chapter connects the teachers' movement to the broader wave of digitally enabled protest in recent years through their shared activist imaginary. Together, these movements have envisioned a world in which the public interest is guarded against continued encroachment by the market logics that have become hegemonic in the neoliberal epoch. Owing to the success of early movements in this wave, activists often romanticized the potential of the Internet, believing that its horizontal structures could manifest in egalitarian, non-hierarchical future societies. Movements like Occupy and the *Indignados* eschewed formal organizations and refused to engage with political systems that they saw as hopelessly captured by neoliberal logics. As a result, the public gatherings slowly died out without any notable policy changes being made. This is where teacher activists have succeeded, as they are anchored to institutions like their schools and unions. In Bennett and Segerbeg's (*The logic of connective action: Digital media and the personalization of contentious politics*. Cambridge, University Press, New York, 2013) formulation, the teachers benefited from both the adaptability of "crowd-enabled mobilizations" and the endurance of "organizationally enabled mobilizations." While the mobilization of broader publics provided the show of public support necessary to build momentum around specific issues, the union architecture provided teacher activists the legitimacy and organizing capacity lacking in other movements in this wave of contestation.

Keywords Global Social Justice Movement · Occupy movement · Indignados · Black Lives Matter · Radical horizontalism · Hybrid movements

One of the defining characteristics of the "movements of the squares" is the spectacle of crowds gathering in mass demonstrations in public squares. These crowds represent a real-world manifestation of the online connections made between activists around common cause, animated by the emotional resonance elicited by the social media platforms in which these movements took shape. The gatherings in squares and streets symbolize the alienation and resentment that has grown in the neoliberal epoch among various sectors of society, especially the young and dispossessed that have gathered during the *Occupy*, *Indignados*, *Black Lives Matter*, and *Arab Spring* protests. I contend that the same forces undergird the teachers' movement, given that it is built around connections between a workforce that has been systematically displaced through decades of neoliberal reforms that have stripped teachers of autonomy while rendering them ever more precarious in their quotidian existence.

It is the crowds that have attracted the attention of the news media, and, by extension, the broader public. As a result, these public displays have served to place educational issues on the discursive agenda, while also helping to build the widespread public support that teacher activists have enjoyed throughout this struggle. However, crowds alone do not gain victories in struggle. For that, movements must build enduring structures to sustain the pressure they are bringing upon those in power. And it is in this regard that the teachers have succeeded where the other movements in this wave have faltered.

In this chapter, I argue that the power of the teachers' movement stems from its hybrid organizational form combining both the crowd-oriented mobilizations of new social movements with traditional union-based organization. Teacher activists have used their formal union architecture to advocate on their behalf at the collective bargaining table, while also incorporating community groups into their ambit and using social media platforms to help connect a larger networked public. I further contend that this combination of organizational and communicative tactics has marked the beginnings of a sectoral shift in the dominant mode of contention among educators in the direction of "social movement unionism."

Lastly, I argue that this approach has been particularly efficacious in terms of building a mass movement with the ability to sustain itself and evade the problem of ephemerality that has plagued other movements in this cycle. In this regard, activist teachers have broken with the neo-anarchism that has animated other movements in this wave, which have tended to embrace prefigurative politics privileging non-hierarchical forms critical of traditional movement organizations.

The Roots of the Digital Activist Imaginary

The "movements of the squares" were born of a crisis of public trust in governing institutions, which activists tended to view as narrowly representing elite interests at the expense of the broader public. Against the backdrop of this mistrust, the Internet emerged as a space that allowed the activist imaginary to flourish, with hopes that the networking affordances of these new communication technologies could be used to empower people that felt disenfranchised and marginalized.

This shared imaginary was particularly prevalent in the early movements in this cycle, as activists embraced a prefigurative politics in which the horizontality of the web would manifest in society as a whole (Gerbaudo, 2012; Wolfson, 2014). Activists drew inspiration from the early success of digitally enabled movements explicitly targeting the neoliberal consensus. One particularly notable example occurred on New Year's Day in 1994, when the Zapatistas, a balaclava-wearing peasant army, occupied several towns and cities in the southern Mexican state of Chiapas in protest of the North American Free Trade Agreement (NAFTA), which went into effect that day. Movement organizers, including the enigmatic Subcomandante Marcos, successfully employed the nascent technologies of the Internet to great effect, mobilizing thousands of people throughout the globe to provide material and financial support: an unthinkable reality just a few years prior.

In countries of the global north, activists used these same communication tools, including emails and message boards, to mobilize and coordinate protests against various meetings of international trade and financial organizations. Some notable examples include the demonstrations at the ministerial meeting of the World Trade Organization in Seattle in 1999 (the so-called "Battle of Seattle") and the annual meetings of the World Economic Forum in Davos, Switzerland. Activists targeted these meetings because they saw them as emblematic of how popular sovereignty had been eroded at the hands of the global economic elite.

In these emergent technologies, activists also saw the potential to circumvent the commercially dominated news media and its stranglehold on the dissemination of news and information. This is the logic that gave rise to Indymedia, a global network of activist-run news sites designed to cover stories that the corporate press ignores (Pickard, 2006; Wolfson, 2014). Activists would use the site to write and post stories about local struggles and to read up on movements in places throughout the world. To a certain extent, this focus on building movement-oriented communications infrastructure worked. For example, the anti-Iraq War movement grew precipitously at the same time, thanks in part to the ability of activists to network on sites like Indymedia. After just a few short months of mobilization, millions of people were marching in hundreds of cities throughout the world. It took several years for the anti-Vietnam War movement to realize such massive public displays. And while activists were unable to stop the Bush Administration from commencing its military action against Iraq, there was a feeling among activists that they had at least won hearts and minds, and that they had broken the stranglehold of elites on media and communication systems. The techno-utopianism of the radical imaginary had reached new heights.

However, this romanticization of the power of networks blinded many activists to the material realities they were operating in. While these new digital communication technologies provided the technological capacity to connect people in far-flung locations around common cause (which is no small thing), there was no "cyberspace" in which dreams of a leaderless future could manifest into reality. In fact, the Internet was never really an egalitarian or "horizontal" space, as it is built upon infrastructure developed by massively profitable corporate entities that rely upon the subjugation of users to the dictates of algorithmically driven platforms. The user data generated by social media platform users—including those organizing radical movements of resistance—constitute the raw material exploited by these platforms to generate spectacular wealth for their owners. Social media companies like Facebook parent company Meta make billions of dollars annually by rendering this data as behavioral prediction products in what Shoshana Zuboff (2019) sees as the basis of "surveillance capitalism": a mode of production based upon subjugating end users to the "instrumentarian power" of tech companies such as Meta and Google parent company Alphabet.

At the same time, activist fixation with leaderless structures has generally contributed to the rapid destabilization of these movements. Many participants have felt that the political system was hopelessly captured by the interests of the elite, the banks, and major multinational corporations, and engaging with such a broken system would make them complicit in some way. As such, they have eschewed the creation of formal organizational structures and any engagement with formal political processes. Hardt and Negri (2004) employ the term "multitude" to describe the resulting form: a distributed network of disparate activists linked around common cause, spread across different geographic locations, workplaces, and advocacy organizations. They liken the multitude to a swarm, acting in concert without any central authority guiding the movement: a formation that they embrace.

Meanwhile, Wolfson (2014), in describing what he terms the "cyber left," views this lack of central authority as a serious flaw in contemporary organizing. Because activists have tended to idealize the network model of the platforms from which they took shape, they have eschewed hierarchies in their group formations. Wolfson contends that this brand of prefigurative politics lacks the organizational structure with which to sustain political pressure and realize meaningful gains: an argument rendered ever more compelling by the fact that the subject of his study—Indymedia—has ceased to exist.

I endorse Wolfson's critique of this radical horizontality. While I believe that Hardt and Negri's characterization of the nature and form of contentious politics in the contemporary age is accurate, their embrace of decentralization is highly problematic. It is perfectly understandable to raise criticisms of existing hierarchies and authorities within social movement organizations, but a wholesale dismissal of any formal organization tends to undermine the durability of movements.

Teachers have not been immune to this frustration with existing institutions, as many have expressed displeasure with the complacency of their union organizations in the face of decades of these neoliberal reforms. However, most of these criticisms have been tempered by an appreciation for the fact that the unions, as a whole, provide the necessary material and institutional support to allow movements to sustain beyond the initial protest actions.

It is here that the teachers' movement breaks with these other movements. They are not operating "outside of the system," given their location within a core cultural institution with legally recognized representation in their unions. I argue that this firm structural foundation is what has rendered the teachers' movement particularly strong and enduring. The ephemerality of the other movements in this wave of contestation has been their biggest weakness, as their narrow reliance on the networking affordances of social media has kept them alive only as long as they have trended enough for the algorithms to keep them afloat.

Nonetheless, I still categorize the teachers' movement among this broader wave of contestation, because they have mobilized support outside of formal union channels in order to change the inner workings thereof. I contend that this is very much in keeping with the spirit of "movements of the squares," described by Gerbaudo (2017) as aspiring to a "government of and by the people, enshrined in all democratic constitutions, yet too often betrayed by the oligarchic distortions of existing democracies" (p. 63). He remarks on the existence of a fundamental tension with the movements between its radically horizontal, anarchistic organizing ethos and its desire to work within governing structures through the demand for popular sovereignty. For teachers, this tension manifested in the form of conflict within the union between its leadership and the rank-in-file. Even in the case where the union leadership led the strike effort—that is, in Chicago in 2012 and 2019—it was the militant CORE slate leading to battle after coming to power on promises of reversing the neoliberal drift of the previous union leadership and the national-level union structures (the two major trade union organizations for teachers, the AFT and the NEA) (Ashby & Bruno, 2016; Brogan, 2013, 2014; Lipman, 2011). In this sense, CORE is still an outside-inside movement-oriented organization, even if it is situated within the inside of the union machinery at the local level.

The teachers took action, at least in part, due to a belief that their unions had betrayed them by acquiescing to the decades' long neoliberal assault on their profession. The example from the Oklahoma Teachers United (OTU) page below evinces this phenomenon, as teachers are asked to reject the American Federation of Teachers (AFT) leadership's acquiescence at the bargaining table.

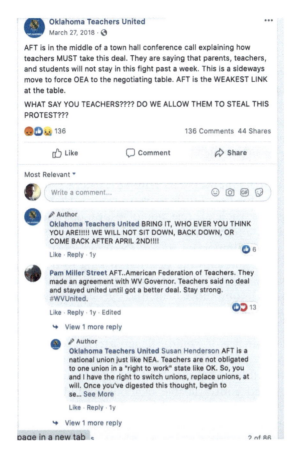

Despite this tension, the existence of the union structure helped the teachers' movement succeed where its predecessors in this wave of protest fell short: in realizing demonstrable material gains through engagement with governing structures. While all of the various state and local efforts fell short of their demands, they, nonetheless, managed substantial concessions that exceeded what would have been possible without the movement.

And this is because criticisms of union governance did not rise to the level of eschewing all organizational structures or over-romanticizing crowds. While no movements succeed without gathering crowds, they also will not endure based solely on the energy those crowds create. Similarly, movements do not benefit from an idealization of the perceived horizontality of networks, since the algorithms driving content privilege that which is new and trending, rather than that which helps build sustaining organizations. In this regard, Jodi Dean (2019) writes, "social media functions to dissipate efforts to hold open the gap produced by the crowd rupture, so that what for a moment was the people is later forgotten, diminished, reinterpreted. Yet its very processes produce new crowd forms through which collectivity tries to exert its force" (p. 179).

There is a valuable lesson to be gained from the teachers in this respect. While it is important to critique existing systems of representative democracy for how much they are captured by elite interests and neoliberal logics, a wholesale rejection of institutions does nothing to help the people whose interests these movements purport to represent. Moreover, leaders play an important role in social movement organizations by providing stability and allowing decision-making to be delegated, rather than having every decision subjected to a tedious deliberative process. In the case of the Occupy movement, the "general assemblies" presented an extreme example of the problems with leaderless decision-making, as participants would spend countless hours debating trivial issues, thus exhausting the patience of would-be supporters.

Formal social movement organizations also provide legitimacy to movements that force people in power to take them seriously. Having a legally registered entity capable of lobbying and bargaining allows a movement to enter the prescribed bounds of political deliberation while bestowing formal legal rights upon the movement to make real demands of political leaders.

Without this kind of institutional legitimacy, movements are reduced to the mobilization of crowds: an essential though insufficient component to any mass movement. Gathering throngs of supportive people together is undoubtedly important to demonstrate popular support. Crowds have the capacity to inspire and energize supporters, providing what French sociologist Emile Durkheim calls "collective effervescence": a sort of cathartic release that comes from participating in a public display of mass solidarity.

Strong movement structures permit this collective expression to effectively address the material realities experienced by the subjects of movements. By having their union bodies advocating for them, the teachers' movement has realized significant gains in most of the locales that an uprising has taken place. This perceived legitimacy also extended to the news media, which took the teacher uprising much more seriously than other recent movements. And it is not just unions that have provided organizational stability and legitimacy to teacher activists. Teachers have also benefited from the existence of community organizations tying them to parents and concerned neighbors and other members of the communities they work in, especially in Chicago, where the CTU has emphasized such alliance building. This cultivation of broader publics has further cemented the institutional footing of this movement.

While the unions allowed teachers to gain the level of legitimacy they needed to succeed with their demands, the social media mobilization allowed the teachers to rally support for demands that went further than anything on the current union agenda. In Bennett and Segerberg's (2013) formulation, the teachers benefited from both the endurance of "organizationally enabled mobilizations" as well as the adaptability of "crowd-enabled mobilizations." In short, the "crowd" was able to check one of the core weaknesses of organizationally driven movements: that they had gotten complacent over the years of neoliberal retrenchment, while also severely restricted by formal legal restrictions put in place limiting the scope of what they could bargain around. These two sides to the movement worked in symbiosis to provide responsiveness to the base (the crowds) and institutional stability.

A Hybrid Movement

Teacher activists have expanded their unions' scope in terms of the issues being addressed, the organizational and communicative tactics employed, and the people being advocated for. They have engaged old union organizing tactics as well as new social movement tactics to connect the broader community around common grievances both online and offline. In this sense, I argue that this is a "hybrid movement," analogous to Chadwick's (2013) concept of a "hybrid media system," which he defines as being "built upon interactions among older and newer media logics – where logics are defined as technologies, genres, norms, behaviors and organizational forms – in the reflexively connected fields of media and politics" (p. 4).

By extension, one can conceive of a "hybrid movement" as one that embraces logics from older movements as well as those of the digital era. Rather than confining a movement to the narrow domain of one form of media and its associated repertoire of contention, the movement engages various tactics from different repertoires of contention and makes use of their associated organizational capacities and media practices. Such an approach largely dodges the various problems associated with the fetishization of one form of media and its undergirding logics, as described by Wolfson (2014) with regard to Indymedia, but which could be extended to Occupy and the other "movements of the squares." The institutional anchor provided by the union organization also helped avoid the problem of ephemerality that has plagued the other movements in this wave of contestation.

While these networking affordances were vital to the movement taking shape when and how it did, I hold that this institutional anchor of the union allowed the movement to succeed in realizing the type of concrete material gains largely lacking from other movements in this wave. In this vein, the "old" and "new" social movement forms effectively worked in symbiosis. By using Facebook for specific functions that permitted networking across districts and in the communities surrounding the participating schools, the teachers' movement was able to fill in the advocacy gap left by decades of relative inaction in the face of the flurry of neoliberal reforms and austerity measures.

I argue that the hybridity of this movement has allowed it to succeed in both the material and discursive arenas: not only have they won contractual victories, but they have also provided an important intervention into larger conversations about the role of education in society. I further argue that this impact is significant because of the centrality of education in the cultural process of incubating the broader hegemonic consensus. It is in schools that people are first exposed to prevailing interpretations of the society around them and the history that has given way to it. Moreover, pupils spend much of their quotidian existence in the care of educators for 12–13 years, thus rendering educational institutions an especially important societal chokepoint in terms of how people view and make sense of the world.

Likewise, media institutions are important for similar reasons. It is through their interfacing with various media forms that people develop their knowledge and understanding of their cultural and political universe. Social media, in particular, represents a central discursive arena in the contemporary media ecology. In order to register as legitimate, movements must have some sort of presence on the major social media platforms.

What makes this the teachers' movement so compelling is that it resides in these two central cultural arenas, effectively contesting neoliberal logics as they manifest in both the techno-social and educational domains. Teacher activists organize on tech platforms that embed neoliberal logics favoring individual over collective action with a narrow focus on profit driven by engagement with algorithmically determined content (Dean, 2019). It is not a space designed to harness collective power, though it has that potential because it needs crowd engagement to be profitable. Likewise, education reforms in recent decades have had the effect of naturalizing a metric-driven neoliberal pedagogy that treats education as instrumental in nature (i.e. as something that is good only insofar as it realizes some other end, rather than being a good in its own right). It is not a space designed for collective organization, though it has that potential because of the presence of so many teachers in close proximity facing the same conditions.

TEACHERS AND THE DIGITAL CITIZENRY

Activists in this wave of contestation exist at the intersection of two of the major forces of the early twenty-first century: neoliberalism and digitization. While these two forces have different origins, they are related due to their historical positioning during the same epoch: a time when finance capital has risen to become dominant, and its logics have become hegemonic and, thus, deeply ingrained in major cultural institutions.

Neoliberalism as a hegemonic ideology places a premium on individual initiative over collective consciousness while privileging lean government and minimal regulation on corporate activity. The individual is idealized as a consumer more so than a citizen or a worker. Dominant media tends to reinforce this consumerist identity, as almost all of the major legacy and digital media are privately run and operated, and, thus, narrowly focused on maximizing advertising revenue.

As such, a certain tension exists between a public that has been highly alienated and the underlying technologies that offer mechanisms of networking and community-building. On the one hand, the public has become ever less connected to civic and political organizations, which formerly served as the primary vehicle of collective action. The decline in traditional civic institutions is well documented by the likes of political scientist Robert Putnam (2000) in his famous book, *Bowling Alone,* who remarks on the decline in formal political organizations as well as more casual neighborhood groups and clubs.

The technological affordances of social media have helped fill that void to a certain degree, creating networks through which a sense of identity can be formed around common purpose and cause. However, the social media platforms, too, are governed by neoliberal logics in which platform feeds are controlled by algorithms that rely on surveillance of user activity to then sell to advertisers as behavioral prediction products (Zuboff, 2019).

I contend that these algorithmic mechanisms of control are analogous to the pedagogical mechanisms of control erected through neoliberal education reforms. In the domain of social media, users are subjected to metric-driven algorithms that dictate what content they are exposed to in the same way that education reformers have sought to narrowly use standardized test scores to determine how education expenditures are distributed. I hold that the objective of neoliberal governance is to use these metrics as disciplinary mechanisms of control. In this regard, I embrace Olssen's (1996) characterization of the subjectivity emergent in the neoliberal epoch, in terms of a shift from a rational "self-interested" individual to a "manipulatable man" that is harnessed by a regime of governance:

> In the shift from classical liberalism to neo-liberalism... there is a... change in subject position from 'homo economicus', who naturally behaves out of self-interest and is relatively detached from the state, to 'manipulatable man', who is created by the state and who is continually encouraged to be 'perpetually responsive'. (p. 340)

While the subject in classical liberalism is rational, the neoliberal subject is rationalized by metric-driven regimes of valuation. Meanwhile, the "contradiction" that emerges in this domain of the digital citizenry is defined by the fact that the monetization of user activity is reliant on networking that can be used to organize movements of resistance. In sum, the "digital citizen" is one controlled by neoliberal valuation schemes, but that is, nonetheless, capable of connecting around common grievances using the networking pathways that are otherwise the raw material of the digital platform companies' profit.

For teachers, the contradictory process plays out on two separate planes: that of the digital citizenry just described and, secondly, that of practitioners of the dominant pedagogical practices of the era. In the latter case, I contend that successive reforms passed at all levels of government have effectively concretized a metric-driven "neoliberal pedagogy" based on standardized test results. In other words, teachers are subjected to neoliberal logics in their working life in the same way that the digital citizen is in their networked social life.

I also argue that this places educators at a critical chokepoint in the system of circulation of neoliberal logics, given the fact that the education is vital to the legitimation and reproduction of ruling logics. The educational realm is arguably even more central to this process than the terrain of media, because of the sheer amount of time that pupils spend at school during their formative years (Althusser, 1971; Gitlin, 2003). As such, these battles over the form and function of education are exceedingly important in terms of understanding the circulation of dominant discourses as well as the counterhegemonic discourses that grow up in response.

By extension, these battles have to do with who we are as a people. The neoliberal project, at its core, has sought to cultivate an obsequious subject that is ill-equipped to fight for its own interest. In the same way that laws limiting the formal right to collectively bargain are designed to close space for working people to advance their own interest, the dominant pedagogy of the neoliberal epoch is one designed to limit the amount of critical thinking and discourse on important social issues occurring in schools, by favoring the banking model of education over the dialogic model.

In other words, teachers have been facing issues that bear on more than just their condition as workers. While recent activism has addressed those contractual issues, such as pay and pensions, they have also had to confront policy that impacts the broader school communities, which, in turn, has called upon teacher activists to wear two hats at once, as advocates for themselves as workers, and as advocates for the larger citizenry captured by neoliberal logics of control.

SOCIAL MOVEMENT UNIONISM

In having to wear multiple hats and embrace a hybrid organizing style, I contend that teacher activists have initiated a shift toward social movement union organizing, through which formal union channels are supplemented with grassroots community organizing (both online and offline).

This shift has been most pronounced in Chicago, where the militant Caucus of Rank-and-File Educators (CORE) slate is now a decade into its leadership of the Chicago Teachers' Union (CTU). After years of relative passivity on the part of the prior union leadership there, CORE acceded to the helm in 2010 on the heels of a grassroots campaign by activists connecting teachers and community members in struggle to contest slated closures of dozens of schools deemed "failing," as well as the larger suite of neoliberal reforms that mandated these closures (Ashby & Bruno, 2016; Brogan, 2013, 2014; Uetricht, 2014). Recognizing that these issues went beyond the bounds of traditional bread and butter issues—e.g. teacher pay and pensions—and instead impacted the broader communities around the schools, activists began cultivating alliances with parents, students, and concerned citizens in those communities (Ashby & Bruno, 2016; Brogan, 2013, 2014; Uetricht, 2014).

Moreover, recent reforms passed in Illinois (as well as most other states) placed severe restrictions on the issues that could be addressed in the formal collective bargaining process. Teachers were legally barred from raising issues outside of compensation and other contractual concerns. Their coalitions with community groups like the Grassroots Education Movement (GEM) have permitted them to inject these issues into the public discourse as a mechanism of circumventing this formal legal blockage. I further contend that this model of organizing was effectively replicated in the 2018–2019 uprising, as teachers in the various states involved in that wave also pushed demands outside of formal union channels through their organizing of broader publics online.

Over the 40–50 years of neoliberal retrenchment preceding this movement, teachers' unions tended to embrace a business unionism model, wherein they narrowly focused efforts on bargaining for the best contract for members without contesting the larger social issues within which they were operating (McCartin et al., 2020; Moody, 1997; Strassfeld & Strassfeld, 2020; Weiner, 2012). This limitation in scope was driven, in part, by a broader tactical shift on the part of unions across all sectors operating in a political climate that became decidedly less favorable to left-wing militancy, and, in part, by formal restrictions implemented through legislative action throughout the country (Moody, 1997; Strassfeld & Strassfeld, 2020). Specifically, state legislatures have enacted significant restrictions on what kinds of issues that teachers' unions are legally permitted to bargain over—usually narrowly related to compensation—while undermining union power with passage of so-called "right to work" legislation in 28 states. The subsequent U.S. Supreme Court decision in *Janus vs. AFSCME, Council 31* effectively extended "right to work" logics beyond the 28 states that formally passed such legislation by declaring fees from non-members to public employee unions unconstitutional.

Teacher activists in recent years have contested this predominance of business unionism by transforming the organizational and communicative model with which they have engaged the larger publics involved in education: not just other teachers, but students, parents, and community members. This change of communicative practice has involved the construction of new networked counter-publics to discuss issues and advocate around them in ways that the existing union architecture was failing to do. With business unionism, the rank-and-file is rarely consulted upon or mobilized to action, which significantly weakens its collective organizing power. Through a combination of organizing at the shop level, the recruitment of school liaisons, and the deployment of the networking affordances of social media, teacher activists have been able to build networks that, at times, have been larger than what the formal union had at its disposal. Meanwhile, teacher activists have networked with the general public including parents and other community members in an effort to connect education-related issues to larger issues around social inequities as they manifest in the educational domain.

Changes in communicative practice also bear on organizational dynamics. The inclusion of broader publics within the communicative ambit, in turn, has been accompanied by a shift in union structure, and is ultimately "interwoven with the question of union democracy and leadership accountability" (Moody, 1997, p. 60). More engagement with the community also typically involves greater reliance on rank-and-file members to do the recruitment and outreach, rather than hired organizers and bureaucrats (Moody, 1997). However, it is important to recognize that this phenomenon is not entirely new: if anything, it is a return to the organizational practice that was dominant prior to the rise to prominence of business unionism during the neoliberal epoch (McAlevey, 2019; Moody, 1997).

This reversion to broader community engagement has, in turn, permitted union activists to address a range of issues outside of traditional bread and butter union demands. Among the issues advocated in this framework of "organizing for the common good" include increased levels of education funding; hiring more support staff and mental health professionals; opposing planned school closures and the concomitant shift to so-called "choice" schools such as charter schools; and demanding that attention be given to infrastructural issues such as decrepit facilities and inadequate textbooks and supplies.

These communicative and organization "fixes" to the prevailing union model are largely in line with the concept of "social movement unionism" (SMU), which Moody (1997) defines as such: "Unions take an active lead in the streets, as well as in politics. They ally with other social movements but provide a class vision and content that make for a stronger glue than that which usually holds electoral or temporary coalitions together" (p. 59).

This pivot in the direction of SMU has been a necessary and inevitable response to conditions created in the educational sector through the decades-long period of neoliberal policymaking. Above, I briefly referenced some of these policies as they pertained to severely restricting the scope of what issues teachers' unions could legally bargain around, essentially formalizing a limited version of business unionism in practice. At the same time, reformers enacted myriad policies that expanded the number of issues directly impacting the lived realities of teachers and students. These include the legalization of so-called choice schools—both charters and voucher programs in which public funds are used for non-traditional programs—as well as the policies of neglect that stripped schools of requisite resources like school aids, nurses, and infrastructure, while at the same time tying the fate of schools and teachers to evaluative metrics, such as the results of standardized test scores. This combination of narrowing the range of bargainable issues coupled with the expanding scope of policy bearing on teachers led them to have little choice but to act outside of the prescribed bounds: by engaging in illegal wildcat strikes, on the one hand, and by organizing among the broader community of people impacted by these reforms.

I argue that the Chicago Teachers' Union has played a central role in this process because it was the first major union to undergo this transformation, and subsequently inspired teacher activists in various locales involved in the rolling uprisings of 2018–2019. As such, the story of Chicago as a microcosm of this broader struggle is absolutely vital: in terms of the history of neoliberal reforms and the history of the CTU's resistance efforts.

CORE activists within the CTU emphasized recruitment of rank-and-file members to become more involved in decision-making through on-site recruitment efforts. One such member, Rebecca Garelli, was recruited out of the local Chicago school she worked at in 2010 by a member of the steering committee for the union's black caucus. While she was previously involved with the local school council, she had never been involved in union politics before then. She subsequently relocated to the Phoenix area and ultimately found herself as a centerpiece of organizing efforts in Arizona's #redfored movement, in which tens of thousands of teachers participated in walkouts, marches, and sickouts in what became the largest teacher strike in that state's history. The insight she brought from her experience in Chicago was invaluable in teaching her the importance of building alliances within the community as part of the united front organizing tactic. In discussing her perception about the relationship of schools to the broader community, she says:

> I think of the role of school as a community hub. And maybe that's from where I'm from in Chicago. And maybe that's, that's the types of schools I've worked in, in title one communities. They're the soul and the heart of the community. They are what drive the community to uplift itself.
>
> And so broadly speaking, that's how I view that role of education. The school is the hub of the community. Not only do we educate, we provide things that they may or may not have and then uplift them. If they, they there's, there's a need, we fill that need, whether it's language, resources, tools, knowledge, technology, internet.
>
> That's how I see schools. It's not just you go to school, you get an education. It's... "I'm embedded in this, this fabric of this community. And we all help each other and work to uplift us all." So to me, it's, it's that cornerstone of our democratic society.

This ethos stands in stark contrast to an existing union structure—the Arizona Education Association (AEA)—that had become largely confined to the world of lobbying on behalf of its members. Another key organizer in Arizona, Derek Harris, describes how ill-equipped the AEA was in terms of building the kind of foundation that CORE established in Chicago. While there were a few staffers with some logistical knowledge on how to run a strike, they did not have the more expansive skill set in building strong community connections.

Most activists involved in the 2018 walkouts characterized their relationship to their unions in similar terms as Harris: cordial, even if many teachers had grown frustrated with the severe limitations and passivity of their unions. However, one prominent figure involved with the Oklahoma movement, Larry Cagle, struck a brashly antagonistic posture in his depiction of the role of the major union organizations in this struggle:

> We were coordinating without the union... The union did not support, and that's not just a local statement. That is a national statement. The national unions did not see this coming... The American Federation of Teachers did not see this wave coming. And as West Virginia rolled out, they wanted to get this wave under control. As they saw Oklahoma coming forward, the unions really pushed back hard. They did not want this to happen. And they said to me explicitly, do you have any idea how much this will cost us a day to have a union action?

He is adamant that, despite formal gestures of support from the national union leadership for the teacher walkouts, they were acting reluctantly. He also assures me that if they followed their union's lead, teachers would never have realized success in securing a pay raise via an increase in the gross production tax on oil and gas revenue. Likewise, Harris feels that Arizona teachers could have accomplished more with their efforts if they had the time or capacity to build the deep community structures that were lacking with the pre-existing union organization. While teachers won a 20% increase in pay over the three-year period beginning after the strike in addition to guarantees of increased education funding, though they have not been able to raise the array of other issues—such as challenges to charter authorizations and school closures—that CORE has organized around. Moreover, even after the 20% increase, Arizona's level of teacher pay remains among the lowest in the country, according to a report by Arizona School Personnel Administration Association.

Indeed, most of the individual 2018–2019 uprisings focused attention on teacher pay, pensions, and education funding: other issues were largely at the periphery. Nonetheless, like the CTU strikes of 2012 and 2019, the "red state rebellion" uprisings of 2018 framed their movement in terms of the common good as well: making sure to align the fate of teachers and students with the broader community. The chart below summarizes the gains realized in each of the locations engaged in strike activity. Teacher pay raises were passed in West Virginia, North Carolina, and Oklahoma.

Meanwhile, in Kentucky, teachers successfully fought off an attempt to overhaul their pension system by moving from a defined benefit system to a hybrid model (Strassfeld & Strassfeld, 2020, p. 347).

The Kentucky pension overhaul was packaged into the sewerage bill in the 11th hour discussed at the beginning of the introductory chapter: legislative trickery that drove thousands of Kentucky educators into the streets, even in the most conservative parts of the state. The fact that teachers had such success in a highly red state like Kentucky points to another shortcoming of how business unionism has often been conducted in such environments. Sarah Gump, an ESL teacher in Madison County, makes precisely this point, noting that the Kentucky Education Association (KEA) operates under a tight political calculus whereby they assume they have to be more tepid in their activism when Republicans are a dominant force in politics. She is also highly involved with SOS Kentucky, a group that has helped to successfully fight back efforts to implement charter schools in Kentucky, which remains one of only seven states without any charter schools. For her, public schools are vital community centers, and she believes people across the political spectrum see them that way, as she enumerates the various roles they play in society:

> I think [education] provides the foundation for having a productive life as an individual, as a citizen, as a future leader. I think, here in Kentucky, we're a poor state generally, but it's amazing the things our schools do. I mean, our schools fed people all during COVID. The family resource centers and our schools help people pay light bills and make sure people have clothes. And some schools... provide a lot of services to the community, whether it's health-related or laundry or social skills and counseling. And I just feel like, especially in Kentucky, they're just the foundation of the community as a major employer.

This discussion illuminates the ways schools serve as the nuclei of communities, even when the extra effort is not made to forge connections in the manner of CORE activists. It also serves as an instructive commentary on the cross-ideological appeal of public schools as bedrocks of the community.

Facebook and a New Repertoire of Contention

While the early movements of this wave of contestation shared a digital imaginary that envisioned a nebulous alternative to the neoliberal order coming to life in the nascent world of cyberspace, contemporary activists organize in the more defined world of social media platforms like Facebook to grow their networked public. Notwithstanding the various problems with Facebook and its algorithms designed to render behavioral data for advertising sales and behavioral prediction products (Zuboff, 2019), it is a useful tool for connecting like-minded people via groups and for inviting and recruiting interested parties to events. Rebecca Garelli, whose lessons about community organizing gained in her Chicago days, also witnessed the power in digital organizing, when she started the group "Arizona Teachers United," and, within two days, it had grown to over 1,500 members. She elaborates:

> I wasn't even a big Facebooker at the time. I'm not like a master Facebooker... and I have three little kids at home, tiny kids at the time, and I'm not paying attention to the page and it just exploded. And I'm going, 'wait a minute!' And that's actually where I met Noah Karvelis, Dylan Wagela and Derek Harris... and they were kind of the loudest voices.

As all involved are quick to point out, that group did not perform any of the legwork involved in building the network of school liaisons, communicating with the news media and planning out the logistics of the various actions they took. Vanessa Arredondo, one of the initial nine core activists involved in organizing the Arizona actions, describes the dynamics of the liaison-building work, in which representatives were recruited at both the school and district level:

> We created a Google form and we asked for liaisons for anybody that wanted to be involved and to share information with their staff... I then created a list with all the school names and all the districts. And I would highlight this list with whoever had a liaison.

> So to this day, I have a lot of people seeing that list and seeing if they know somebody at that school to be able to help them organize and then to work together as a district liaison.

This liaison building was a vital part of the organizational intervention teacher activists have made as part of this movement, especially in Chicago and Arizona. It allowed for sustained pressure to be brought to bear in the form of successive walkouts, pickets, and mass rallies. Moreover, this real-world organizing served to amplify the networking affordances of Facebook, by allowing them to bring ever more people into their Facebook group, which, in turn, allowed for bigger actions to take place.

It also helped provide power in numbers beyond what the formal union organizations had, weakened as they were by right to work laws and other legal strictures discussed earlier in this chapter. In this regard, Oklahoma Teachers United (OTU) lead organizer Larry Cagle notes, "Our group has 40,000 people in it, but there are only 12,000 union members, which means we can talk to more teachers than the union ever could."

At the same time, Facebook allowed individual activists to share stories about their organizing efforts across their respective states in what amounted to collective acts of motivation (discussed in greater detail in Chapter 6). Seeing what other teacher activists were doing—in terms of the signs they were making and holding at pickets, what messages they were communicating, what ideas they had for future organizations— helped to motivate other supporters in the same Facebook group (be it a statewide group or a district or county-based group). On this account, Arredondo elaborates:

> I remember those first days the group: it just grew by the thousands within the first week. And it just kept growing and growing and growing. And we had this platform that allowed us to communicate with, educators across the state.... People everywhere, tagging everything that was going on in their districts.

Facebook proved to be such a valuable tool for movement activists, in part, because of the presence of features like "groups" and "events," which facilitate movement organization, but also because of the sheer popularity of the platform. It continues to have the biggest user base of any social media platform in the United States, despite recent declines. Gerbaudo (2012) explains, "What makes this medium so effective for drawing people in, including those with no previous experience of political participation, is the fact that it allows activists to tap into people's "real" social networks... many of those my interviewees interact with on

Facebook were indeed their real friends or close acquaintances, rather than 'Facebook friends.'"

In other words, it is not direct engagement with weak ties that makes Facebook so powerful an organizing tool as much as the access to other people's strong ties: the fact that content can be passed on through a chain of close friendships until it reaches the majority of a given community—such as teachers in a school district—in relatively short order. Previously, connecting across these social circles for purposes of political organizing was tedious and time-consuming.

Building support through shared narratives is a defining characteristic of digitally enabled social movements. Bennett and Segerberg (2013) describe this repertoire of contention as "connective action," characterized by the use of "personal action frames" to connect through common lived experiences. In the case of the Occupy movement, for example, activists shared stories of their economic struggles using "we are the 99%," or similar phrases, to connect around common narratives. Similarly, in Chapter 6, I inspect the specific ways that teacher activists used Facebook in greater detail, ultimately finding that activists tended to begin with posts that I categorize as "narration of cause."

Another important facet of organizing via social media is that it helps insulate people from the awkwardness that would normally accompany the act of approaching friends' friends with political causes. On Facebook and other social media platforms, one need not direct any given post at a specific individual, as all content gets incorporated into the newsfeed. Furthermore, all manner of content is commingled in social media feeds, so that there is not a special station for politics and activism. Thus, posts providing information about a teachers' rally appear in the same stream as everything else. Not only does this contribute to insulating users from the uneasiness they might feel with political posts, but it also helps shield activists from censorship, in what Ethan Zuckerman (2013) refers to as the "cute cat theory" of activism, arguing: "Internet tools designed to let ordinary consumers publish non-political content are often useful for activists because they are difficult for governments to censor without censoring innocuous content" (para. 5).

As mentioned above, it is also highly problematic for activists to rely on platforms designed by tech companies seeking to maximize revenue through engagement with algorithmically driven content. These algorithms tend to favor content that elicits strong emotional responses rather than content that dispassionately informs the public on important matters.

Moreover, the routine surveillance of user activity by these platform companies raises a host of ethical concerns, including the potential for abuse by malicious third parties. Lastly, the leaders that emerge in online groups are often not the best organizers in real life, which can contribute to the destabilization that often visits digitally enabled movements.

Nonetheless, there is also power to be gained from the networking affordances of social media. Movements gain power from their numbers, and social media is a tool that can facilitate the growth of those numbers around specific organizing initiatives. However, it is important that activists have intent in their use of social media. In Chapter 6, I show how Facebook was a place for discussion of issues, articulation of the underlying cause, and mobilization of followers. It allowed for the growth of the movement out of shared narratives and common grievances. It also allowed for teachers to connect with a broader public of concerned citizens interested in defending public education.

Teacher power in the digital age stems from the unique capacity of teachers to turn crowds into lasting movements. This power is built on the numbers that they have in their ranks, in addition to their connection to communities forged through the vital service that they provide. And this power renders teachers uniquely capable of contesting neoliberalism in two of its most important domains of legitimation: digital media and education. In a historical moment that is otherwise defined by the ephemerality of crowds and social media trends, teachers represent one of the last vestiges of a profession deeply tied to community structures in a way that allows for meaningful and sustained contestation.

References

Althusser, L. (1971/2014). *On the reproduction of capitalism: Ideology and ideological state apparatuses*. Verso.

Ashby, S., & Bruno, R. (2016). *A fight for the soul of public education: The story of the Chicago teachers strike*. Cornell University Press.

Bennett, L., & Segerberg, A. (2013). *The logic of connective action: Digital media and the personalization of contentious politics*. Cambridge, University Press.

Brogan, P. (2013). Education in global Chicago and the remaking of contemporary capitalism. *The Canadian Geographer/Le Geographe canadien, 57*(3), 303–310.

Brogan, P. (2014). Getting to the CORE of the Chicago Teachers' Union transformation. *Studies in Social Justice, 8*(2), 145–164.

Chadwick, A. (2013). *The hybrid media system*. Oxford University Press.

Dean, J. (2019). Critique or collectivity? Communicative capitalism and the subject of politics. In D. Chandler and C. Fuchs (Eds.), *Digital objects digital subjects: Interdisciplinary perspectives on capitalism, labour and politics in the age of big data* (pp. 171–182). London: University of Westminster Press.

Gerbaudo, P. (2012). *Tweets and the streets: Social media and contemporary activism*. Pluto Press.

Gerbaudo, P. (2017). *The mask and the flag: Populism, citizenism and global protest*. Oxford University Press.

Gitlin, T. (2003). *The whole world is watching: Mass media in the making and unmaking of the new left*. The University of California Press.

Hardt, M., & Negri, A. (2004). *Multitude: War and democracy in the age of Empire*. The Penguin Press.

Lipman, P. (2011). *The new political economy of urban education: Neoliberalism, race, and the right to the city*. Routledge.

McAlevey, J. (2019, June 5). Traditional organizing is not failing. *Boston Review*. www.bostonreview.net

McCartin, J., Sneiderman, M., & BP-Weeks, M. (2020). Combustible convergence: Bargaining for the common good and the #redfored uprisings of 2018. *Labor Studies Journal, 45*(1), 97–113.

Moody, K. (1997). Towards an international social movement unionism. *New Left Review, 225*, 52–72.

Olssen, M. (1996). In defense of the welfare state and of publicly provided education. *Journal of Education, 11*(3), 337–362.

Pickard, V. (2006). Assessing the radical democracy of Indymedia: Discursive, technical and institutional constructions. *Critical Studies in Media Communication, 23*(1), 19–38.

Putnam, R. D. (2000). *Bowling Alone: The Collapse and Revival of American Community*. Simon and Schuster, New York.

Strassfeld, N., & Strassfeld, R. (2020). After Janus: Teachers' unions, walkouts, and social justice unionism. *International Journal of Education Reform, 29*(4), 334–353.

Uetricht, M. (2014). *Strike for America*. Verso.

Weiner, L. (2012). *The future of our schools: Teachers unions and social justice*. Haymarket Books.

Wolfson, T. (2014). *Digital rebellion: The birth of the cyber left*. University of Illinois Press.

Zuboff, S. (2019). *The age of surveillance capitalism: the fight for a human future at the new frontier of power*. New York: PublicAffairs.

Zuckerman, E. (2013). Cute cats to the rescue? Participatory media and political expression. In D. Allen & J. Light (Eds.), *Youth, new media and political parties*.

CHAPTER 3

Teachers in the Material Reality

Abstract This chapter looks at the economic and political context in which the teachers' movement emerged, focusing on recent education reforms and the rhetoric that was used to legitimate them. This history starts with the Reagan administration's employment of alarmist rhetoric in a policy paper entitled "A Nation at Risk," which claimed that the country was falling behind countries like Germany and Japan in industrial dynamism because of the ineptitude of its schools and teachers. The disciplinary language set the groundwork for education policy that emphasized high-stakes standardized tests as a mechanism to hold schools and teachers accountable over the next few decades. At the federal level, this process culminated in the passing of No Child Left Behind and Race to the Top under the second Bush and Obama administrations, respectively. At the local level, Chicago played an especially important role as a laboratory for neoliberal education reforms. This chapter charts these reforms, and highlights how they led to the emergence of the militant Caucus of Rank-and-File Educators (CORE) in the Chicago Teachers' Union, which is focused on addressing the threat posed by choice schools to their job stability and professional autonomy.

Keywords Chicago Teachers' Union · Caucus of Rank-and-File Educators · A Nation at Risk · Crisis in education · No Child Left behind · Race to the Top · Bush education policy · Obama education policy

© The Author(s), under exclusive license to Springer Nature Switzerland AG 2025
M. Reichel, *Teacher Power in the Digital Age*, Social Movements and Transformation, https://doi.org/10.1007/978-3-031-87191-7_3

In the previous chapter, I argued that teachers are especially well-positioned to lead broader community movements aimed at pushing back against neoliberal policies of dislocation, while also contesting the undergirding logics that animate the neoliberal project. However, I have only briefly touched upon the nature of those logics and the history that gave birth to neoliberalism as a hegemonic governing project. This chapter is designed to provide more of that history and context, while setting up the discussion in Chapter 5 about how hegemonic logics circulate through various societal sectors.

In the previous two chapters, I have also argued that this wave of contestation is, in part, characterized by the fact that these movements are all born of the structural crisis of neoliberal capitalism. This chapter locates the current historical juncture of crisis and rupture within a longer cycle of capitalist crises and provides a deeper sense of historical context for the emergence of the teachers' movement while highlighting its structural embeddedness. In this respect, I recognize that what is going on in the educational domain is tightly wound up with what is going on in society as a whole. By extension, teachers' movements are naturally part of broader struggles at any given historical juncture.

Specifically, I look at the progression from the Fordist mode of capitalist development into the current mode characterized by neoliberal mechanisms of control. I also elaborate on how the neoliberal subject is routinely monitored and evaluated as part of the underlying disciplinary logics, which have manifested in workplaces throughout the world economy in the form of micro-management and "peer pressure" (Hardt & Negri, 2000; Kumar, 2007).

CENTRAL ASSUMPTIONS OF A CYCLICAL ANALYSIS OF HISTORY

There are three core assumptions underpinning this central argument. The first assumption is that economic cycles are natural parts of capitalist dynamics, defined by one dominant accumulation regime coming into crisis and subsequently being replaced by a new one that responds to the problems underpinning the crisis that emerged.

The second assumption rooting this chapter's analysis is that current social dynamics are largely defined by the most recent notable transition—in the 1970s—from a Fordist to a neoliberal regime of accumulation (Hardt & Negri, 2000; Harvey, 2005; McNally, 2011). There is broad scholarly agreement on the shift from Fordism to neoliberalism as being one of the dominant features of the latter half of the twentieth century, characterized by a set of policies undertaken by the leading global economies to address the profit slump encountered in the 1970s crisis of stagflation. These policies include the mass privatization of public infrastructure, suppression of wages, wholesale attacks on unions, and the "globalization" of production and supply chains in order to exploit cheaper labor in other parts of the world. (Hardt & Negri, 2000; Harvey, 2005; Lipman, 2011; McNally, 2011). Meanwhile, shop floor management moved from Taylorism to what Moody (1997) characterizes as "lean production," which includes the intensification of work processes and the transfer of management duties to monitorial teams (Apple, 1996; Harvey, 2005; Hardt & Negri, 2000; Kumar, 2007; McNally, 2011). What is made to look like flexibility and autonomy in the workplace—with control shifted from centralized management to teams on the shop floor—is actually a mechanism of heightened control and surveillance, what Parker and Slaughter (1988) call "management by stress." Kumar (2007) relates: "Lean production strips workers' control over the shop floor... It uses as few materials as possible, and workers must work as fast as they can to make up for their inadequate numbers. Peer pressure is enormous, because if one worker slows or stops the production process, all the other workers are adversely affected" (27). In this shift to collective surveillance, the neoliberal subject is made to blame herself for her failure to live up to the "standard of self-sufficiency" (Swales et al., 2020).

My third assumption—drawing on the autonomist Marxist tradition—is that there is a concomitant social shift of the dominant subjectivity in response to the emergence of a new regime of accumulation (Hardt & Negri, 2000). The autonomist tradition emerged largely in Italy in the 1960s as a response to the emergence of left-wing movements that no longer centered on the traditional industrial worker as the principal contentious subject. They explain this transition using the Gramscian notion of hegemony, wherein the governing consensus is achieved through a deliberative process operating in the cultural arena. In this process, the elite respond to demands posed from below and restructure institutions while reformulating the mechanisms of exploitation accordingly. The principal restraint of Fordism related to the laboring subject being sequestered in sites of industrial production with their ability to bargain limited to their collevtive power held in withholding labor power within that production site (Hardt & Negri, 2000). In contradistinction, the neoliberal labor market emphasizes notions of "flexibility" that give the neoliberal subject the "freedom" to pursue life outside of the confines of the factory, but that, in practice, have stripped workers of the stability and protections that workers had in the Fordist epoch.

Meanwhile, neoliberal subjects are exposed to a regime of discipline that extends beyond the workplace, a reality that autonomists describe as the "social factory" (Dyer-Witheford, 1999). Entire communities are reshaped by urban planning, development, housing, and education policies in which market logics are privileged over the interests of people in the communities impacted by these policies. As a result, contemporary left-wing movements tend to not be focused on the shop floor as the principal locus of contestation, and instead exist throughout society, raising grievances on different issues in response to neoliberal logics being applied within these different domains of society.

The Crisis of Fordism and Birth of Neoliberalism

The shift from Fordism to neoliberalism occurred due to twin and interrelated economic and social crises that caused capital to seek a new grand bargain with labor, starting with the crisis of stagflation in the late 1970s. Harvey (2005) notes: "In the US, the control of wealth by the top 1 per cent of the population had remained fairly stable throughout the twentieth century. But in the 1970s it plunged precipitously as asset values (stocks, property, savings) collapsed. The upper classes had to move decisively if they were to protect themselves from political and economic annihilation" (15). The boom that followed the shock of the world wars had lost steam, and capital had exhausted its ability to generate sufficient growth through existing avenues (Harvey, 2005; McNally, 2011). With profit rates falling steadily from the mid-1960s through to the late 1970s, the elite raised a counteroffensive on labor and the broader social infrastructure that had been developed in the preceding era. On the net effect of this elite retrenchment, McNally (2011) writes: "It was not just wages that were pushed down… it was also that speed-up and work intensification compelled workers to produce more per hour. And in conditions of labor retreat, such productivity gains were claimed almost entirely by capital, a trend that began in the late 1970s and kept intensifying across the neoliberal period" (p. 48).

At the same time, a social crisis brewed that led to the implementation of new mechanisms of control. At its root, this was a crisis of unions as the principal organ of progressive politics. Organized around the workplace as the fundamental social unit, unions came to be a major political force by the mid-twentieth century, only to expend their mandate in the face of palpable frustration with the pace of change. The worldwide uprising of 1968 was one operating largely outside of union organization, characterized by a desire for more fundamental societal change than unions could realize. Wallerstein (2011) describes this zeitgeist as such: "You have taken state power but have not at all changed the world. If we, the revolutionaries of 1968, wish to change the world, we must replace you with new movements and new strategies. And we shall do this" (77). These revolutionaries were trapped within a liberal political foundation that would defend basic social provisions designed to guarantee a modicum of decency but still trapped them within the same world of work to which their parents belonged (Hardt and Negri, 2000; Wallerstein, 2011).

In the face of Fordist restraint, the 60 s revolutionaries called for "freedom" and "flexibility," which would come to constitute the foundation of the emerging neoliberal order. For Hardt and Negri (2000), this fact is glimpsed in the concomitant collapse of the Soviet Union, built as it was on Fordist logics of worker discipline. In their view, the rising "immaterial economy" of increasingly educated workers could no longer be subjected to such a crude regime of discipline, which ultimately undermined its legitimacy. In the place of Fordism emerged a social organization wherein atomized individuals provide their intellectual and affective capacities for an economy increasingly built around networks and flows (Hardt & Negri, 2000; Harvey, 2005). While many workers might like the arrangement, in principle, for the freedom it permits in organizing one's professional life, this focus on flexibility has also meant transferring the burden of welfare to the individual. The overarching governing logic has been used to legitimize the ongoing assault on the social welfare state by stressing a libertarian ethos of personal responsibility. As a result, one's misfortune is deemed the result of personal failing, rather than structural defects (Harvey, 2005).

In this context, "freedom" takes on a negative rather than a positive formulation. It comes to mean the right to employ one's privilege to whatever ends one chooses, even if it means promulgating harms upon others. In the era where fascists deployed this sense of the word, Polanyi (1954) describes how it "degenerates into a mere advocacy of free enterprise," wherein "the fullness of freedom for those whose income, leisure and security need no enhancing, and a mere pittance of liberty for the people, who may in vain attempt to make use of their democratic rights to gain shelter from the power of the owners of property" (256–258). Neoliberalism embraces this inverted, negative freedom as a mechanism of legitimation for what has, in effect, been an intensification of the industrialization and commercialization that the'60 s rebels rose against. While immaterial workers have, indeed, been increasingly liberated from the confines of the shop floor, they have been unleashed upon a world now immersed in capitalist logics. Mandel (1975) relates, "Mechanization, standardization, overspecialization and parcelization of labor, which in the past determined only the realm of commodity production in actual industry, now penetrate into all sectors of social life… The profitability of universities, music academies and museums starts to be calculated in the same way as that of brick works or screw factories" (p. 387).

The neoliberal subject possesses the "freedom" and "flexibility" to be exploited in all sectors of society and facets of life. If the crisis of Fordism was centered on the shop floor, the crisis of neoliberalism exists anywhere and everywhere. This is because neoliberalism is not simply a set of governing economic principles, but also the social logics that set them in motion. As a governing project, neoliberalism seeks to embed its rationalization scheme into the cultural apparatus. It is for this reason that reformers have singled out education policy as a critical mechanism of control through which capitalist notions of freedom could be naturalized and embedded in the psyche. At the same time, neoliberal mechanisms of discipline and evaluation have been extended to the teaching corps via policies that hold teachers accountable for pupil performance on standardized tests.

The Birth of Neoliberal Education Reforms

Out of the twin crises of the late 1960s and 1970s, the elite project of neoliberal retrenchment was born: one in which flexibility and negative freedom were realized through various schemes of privatization, cutbacks in spending, public–private partnerships, and neo-Taylorist mechanisms of surveillance. In the educational domain, a marriage of convenience emerged between neoliberal reformers that sought to make schools work like markets and conservatives concerned by the gains of the 60 s movements who resented the role educational institutions played as one of the central sites of struggle (MacLean, 2017).

Beginning in the late 70 s, these reformers initiated a discourse that portrayed schools and teachers as failing to live up to standards required to keep the country economically competitive. This discourse was formalized at the national level under the Reagan administration with its publishing of *A Nation at Risk* by education czar, T.H. Bell, which narrowly placed blame for the nation's economic woes on deficient schools and the teachers that were failing to keep student performance up to acceptable standards. This influential document called for education policy that would introduce disciplinary measures to get the education sector into line by penalizing individual schools and teachers for subpar performance on standardized tests (Goldstein, 2014). While these initiatives were ultimately encouraged by national-level legislation, the enactment of these reforms occurred unevenly across various states and municipalities. Typically, though, majority minority communities were singled out for reforms, with Chicago ultimately becoming a laboratory for them during the latter half of the second Richard Daley's mayoralty.

The prevailing economic conditions in Chicago during the last decades of the twentieth century made it particularly ripe for these reforms. Like other cities in the former northern industrial heartland, Chicago's once robust economy had progressively been decimated during the era of white flight and deindustrialization in the post-war years, thus undermining its tax base (Weber, 2010). At the same time, federal urban renewal dollars were drastically cut back during the Reagan years and never subsequently restored (Lipman, 2011). In response, the city turned to finance to fill the gap, through which it pioneered the use of Tax Increment Financing (TIF), a mechanism through which development projects are funded by future property tax revenues funded in the short terms by loans (Weber, 2010).

Over time, the pressure to pay off the underlying loans has effectively caused TIFs to move away from their original urban renewal purpose. Briffault (2010) describes how the notion of what constitutes "blight" has morphed in the eyes of legislatures and courts throughout the country from "the slum image of decayed or deteriorated structures, unsafe and unsanitary conditions, and economic and social distress to something a lot more like 'underdeveloped' or lacking the physical or legal preconditions for further economic development" (p. 78). In Chicago, this change of course was legally effected by a 1999 amendment to the state of Illinois' "TIF-enabling act" to only require that half of the parcels in a district be greater than 35 years old and "potentially blighted in the future" (Weber & O'Neill-Kohl, 2013, p. 203). This amendment has, in turn, led to a re-orientation of TIF allocation from job creation to real estate development. Geographically, the result has been a bias toward projects abutting the "Loop" central business district, which had been previously undervalued due to the presence of barriers like rivers and railways (Weber, 2010).

After years of public pressure over the narrow focus of TIFs on development, officials began channeling these funds into education projects, but generally with a marked preference for "choice" schools (Farmer & Poulos, 2015). For example, the city built six new elite selective enrollment schools starting in the late 90 s to assuage concerns about the quality of the existing system in a period when governing officials were focused on luring in businesses as part of its post-industrial reinvention as a "global city" (Ashby & Bruno, 2016; Farmer & Poulos, 2015). In analyzing data for the year 2010, Farmer and Poulos found that despite only comprising 1% of the schools in the city, the selective enrollment schools received 33% of the expenditures, against 48% allotted to traditional neighborhood schools, which make up 69% of all schools (Farmer & Poulos, 2015, pp. 162–163). While this is just a limited one-year sample, it does nonetheless provide one telling illustration of how TIFs are used to undermine existing community-rooted schools in favor of alternatives based on "performance" and "accountability" (Lipman, 2011).

In sum, the neoliberal turn to finance resulted in a geographic reshaping of the city wherein development was tied to profitability rather than community sustainability. At the local level, these policies comported with Mayor Richard Daley's desire to keep middle-class families in the city by providing attractive education infrastructure (Ashby & Bruno, 2016). Meanwhile, the broader shift in the focus of municipal policy in Chicago reflected a global process wherein government was brought into line with the dictates of global finance. Geographically, this shift has translated into the development of a bifurcation between a hollowed out industrial corridor, on the one hand, and a renovated central business district catering largely to tech and finance workers (Ashby & Bruno, 2016; Castells, 1989; Lipman, 2011; Sassen, 2001).

These "gentrified" areas receive a disproportionate share of the city's education funding through the fact that children from these communities are more likely to be accepted into one of the well-funded and highly regarded magnet schools (Ashby & Bruno, 2016). The rest of the city has, meanwhile, been subjected to chronic underfunding of most schools, outright closures of others, and a shift in resources to largely non-unionized charter schools (Ashby & Bruno, 2016; Lipman, 2011).

From Monitoring to Control

Neoliberal education policy has sought to doubly displace education from its.

role as bedrock of the community: by reshaping urban space to adapt to the needs of global finance and by opening up space for private investors to profit on public education. In practice, Lipman (2011) describes the resulting reforms as marking a move from "government to governance": a shift to a logic of monitoring and controlling populations. In practice, this has meant oversight bodies have been increasingly insulated from public purview and turned over to specialists charged with bringing the school in line with the market principle of "efficiency," largely determined by test-based performance (Lipman, 2011). This restructuring has permitted more fluid streamlining of urban education policy with the mandates of the federal "No Child Left Behind" NCLB law and latterly the "Race to the Top" (RTTP) legislation, through which funding allotments have been tied to performance on standardized tests (Lipman, 2011). For example, in Chicago, the school system was placed under the control of a CEO in 1995. Subsequently, the city passed the "Renaissance 2010" plan in 2006, which called for 60 closings and the opening of 100 alternative, mostly charter, schools, with closure decisions being guided by results of standardized tests (Lipman, 2011).

What is notable about these reforms is not that government assumed the responsibility of evaluating students and teachers so much as the high-stakes nature of the testing regime that resulted. Previous efforts at standardization, such as in the case of the development of the Standard Aptitude Test (SAT), were designed to provide a mechanism to sort students into certain roles within the burgeoning industrial economy (Hartman, 2003). In this context, tests played a disciplinary, rather than a controlling, function in society. Educators retained a good deal of control over pedagogy because the fortunes of the school districts were not directly tied to test results the way they are under current policy (Ashby & Bruno, 2016; Hartman, 2003; Lipman, 2011).

In contradistinction, No Child Left Behind (NCLB) introduced a significant role for the federal government by tying federal funding to the results of standardized tests and allowing parents to send their children to alternative schools if their local public schools are deemed failing by enacted standards. Introduced in the early years of the second Buch administration, NCLB was the culmination of previous efforts by reformers to address the perceived crisis of education by implementing science-based evaluation schemas to ensure "adequate yearly progress" (AYP) in student test scores. Failures to demonstrate improvement in test scores for two years result in a school being deemed "failing," thus allowing parents to seek alternatives elsewhere. After four years of failed improvement, a school is deemed as needing "corrective action," which could mean wholesale replacement of existing teaching staff.

The states retained a prominent role in determining the nature of the standards being assessed, especially in the 2015 amendment to the bill, known as the Every Student Succeed Acts (ESSA), though the federal government still oversees the implementation of those standards. Meanwhile, it is not the content of the standardized tests that matters as much as the fact that they are provided such importance in the broader schema of how the education system functions. From a pedagogical standpoint, these reforms have erected an incentive structure that effectively privileges the banking model of instruction in which teachers play the role of bank tellers depositing information into students (Freire, 1970/2018).

Moreover, these reforms also naturalize a corporatist ideology that dictates that public infrastructure would universally benefit from a dose of market discipline. School districts are subjected to the same "management by stress" that has become fashionable elsewhere in the neoliberal economy, with data-driven results used to ruthlessly govern the way scarce education dollars are earmarked. With the subsequent "Race to the Top" law passed under the Obama administration, this market discipline was extended to the point that teachers could actually be fired as a result of poor performance of their students on standardized tests. In order to qualify for grants under the program, schools had to enact strict "transformations" and "turnarounds" if they failed to meet prescribed standards on test scores. In a transformation, principals are fired and teacher performance is tied to test results, with up to 50% potentially being fired. In a "turnaround," a corporate consultant is brought in to manage the school, with at least 50% of teaching staff having to be dismissed.

The result is an incentive structure that technically gives local schools the freedom to pursue their own preferred methods, but narrows the evaluative bounds so tightly that there, realistically, is not much that schools can do but emphasize teaching to the test as a pedagogical method. With their jobs on the line, teachers are unlikely to experiment with alternative pedagogical methods or to spend time with activities focused on critical thinking and problem-solving. It doesn't matter that teachers technically have "freedom from" interference by government into their pedagogical practice when the disciplinary apparatus is so onerous that they are effectively controlled in their quotidian activity.

Hartman (2003) compares this regime of control to the International Monetary Fund (IMF) within the global economy: a mechanism that forecloses local sovereignty by locking countries into a regulatory framework that privileges financial flows over all else. Technically, governments were not being conquered in the traditional imperial mold, but, in all reality, governments were subject to the dictates of hegemonic economic thinking through their obligation to follow the one-size-fits-all approach of the IMF-mandated structural adjustment programs.

Likewise, with teaching, testing is just one evaluative mechanism that can be employed among others. In the New Deal-era regime of evaluation in which the SAT emerged, the need to engage a varied approach to teaching was still respected. The tests merely served to determine who was worthy of an elite college education (Hartman, 2003). Those scoring poorly on the test were not at risk of having their schools shuttered or handed over to private charter organizations. Moreover, inept teachers were not yet viewed as one of the primary sources of the country's problems, though that idea would soon germinate in mass media portrayals of a school system needing to be brought to heel.

In Chapter 5, I will further elaborate on how discourses blaming teachers for educational problems emerged out of the neoliberal zeitgeist and came to serve as legitimation for the reforms being passed throughout the country. I will also advance a model for better understanding the connection between dominant regimes of governance, the discourses that animate them, the policy that results, and the counterhegemonic movements that develop in response. This heuristic will then be used as a basis for understanding the empirical investigations that follow in the later chapters on media framing of the teachers' movement and activist teachers' response as glimpsed in their social media use.

Before pivoting to that discussion, I will first provide a history of the class, race, and gender dynamics of the teaching profession in the United States. While recent reforms are unique in the ferocity by which metrics are used to manage educators, this is not the first time that disciplinary reforms have been implemented in the education sector. There has long been a paternalistic tendency to education policy, owing to the historically gendered nature of the profession, as an extension of the gendered division of labor in which women are disproportionately consigned to the "unproductive" realm of care work. Understanding this tension between male-dominated politicians managing policy over a female-dominated teaching corps is crucial to then understanding how the mechanisms of control discussed in this chapter have been implemented so successfully.

REFERENCES

Apple, M. (1986). *Teachers and texts: A political economy of class and gender relations in education.* Routledge.

Ashby, S., & Bruno, R. (2016). *A fight for the soul of public education: The story of the Chicago teachers strike.* Cornell University Press.

Briffault, R. (2010). The most popular tool: Tax increment financing and the political economy of local government. *The University of Chicago Law Review, 77*(1), 65–95.

Castells, M. (1989). The informational city: Information technology, economic restructuring, and the urban-regional process. Malden, MA: Blackwell.

Dyer-Witheford, N. (1999). *Cyber-Marx: Cycles and circuits of struggle in high-technology capitalism.* University of Illinois Press.

Farmer, S., & Poulos, C. (2015). Tax increment financing in Chicago, IL, building neoliberal exclusion one school at a time. *Critical Sociology, 41*(1), 153–171.

Freire, P. (2018). *Pedagogy of the Oppressed.* Bloomsbury Publishing. (Original work published 1970).

Goldstein, D. (2014). *The teacher wars: A history of America's most embattled profession.* Doubleday.

Hardt, M., & Negri, A. (2000). *Empire.* Harvard University Press.

Hartman, A. (2003). The social production of American identity: Standardized testing reform in the United States. *Socialism and Democracy, 17*(2), 131–164.

Harvey, D. (2005). *A Brief history of neoliberalism.* Oxford University Press.

Kumar, D. (2007). *Outside the box: Corporate media, globalization, and the UPS strike.* University of Illinois Press.

Lipman, P. (2011). *The new political economy of urban education: Neoliberalism, race, and the right to the city.* Routledge.

MacLean, N. (2017). *Democracy in chains: The deep history of the radical right's stealth plan for America.* Penguin.

Mandel, E. (1975). *Late capitalism.* Verso.

McNally, D. (2011). *Global slump: The economics and politics of crisis and resistance.* PM Press.

Moody, K. (1997). Towards an international social movement unionism. *New Left Review, 225,* 52–72.

Parker, M., & Slaughter, J. (1988). *Choosing sides: Unions and the team concept.* South End Press.

Polanyi, K. (1954). *The great transformation.* Beacon Press.

Sassen, S. (2001). *The global city: New York, London, Tokyo.* Princeton University Press.

Swales, S. et al (2020). Neoliberalism, guilt, shame and stigma: A Lacanian discourse analysis of food insecurity. *Journal of Community and Applied Social Psychology, 30*(6):673–687.

Wallerstein, I. (2011). Dynamics of (unresolved) global crisis. In C. Calhoun & G. Derluguian (Eds.), *Business as usual: The roots of the global financial meltdown.* NYU Press.

Weber, R., & O'Neill-Kohl, S. (2013). The historical roots of tax increment financing, or how real estate consultants kept urban renewal alive. *Economic Development Quarterly, 27*(3), 193–207.

Weber, R. (2010). Selling city futures: The financialization of urban redevelopment policy. *Economic Geography, 86*(3), 251–274.

CHAPTER 4

Teachers in the Broader Struggles Over Class, Race, and Gender

Abstract This chapter turns the focus to longer-running systems of class-, race-, and gender-based domination. In drawing on critical feminist literature—largely from scholars in the Autonomist Marxist tradition, including Federici (2004), Vogel (2013) and Fortunati (1995, 2007)—I look at how this highly feminized nature of teaching work has emerged out of the patriarchal division of labor between the productive and reproductive realm, with women historically relegated to the latter in the un- and under-compensated roles of housewives, care workers, domestic workers, and, ultimately, teachers. I also contend that these class-, race-, and gender dynamics are integral to understanding the battles over education, given that teaching has historically been singled out for disciplinary reforms because of its highly feminized nature.

Keywords Marxist feminism · Autonomist marxism · Reproductive vs productive labor · Gendered division of labor · Feminized nature of teaching · Gendered labor

The previous chapters have situated the teachers' uprising of the last decade in the hegemonic crisis of neoliberal capitalism, arguing that the educational realm has been a central site of struggle in this crisis due its

© The Author(s), under exclusive license to Springer Nature Switzerland AG 2025
M. Reichel, *Teacher Power in the Digital Age*, Social Movements and Transformation, https://doi.org/10.1007/978-3-031-87191-7_4

integral role in the legitimation of ruling logics, as well as the contradictions that inhere in education being part of the evaluative and monitorial apparatus of neoliberalism. Most of the discussion there focused on the logics specific to neoliberalism, rather than longer-running system of domination and exploitation operating in the realm of education. In this chapter, I turn to inspecting those systems: specifically, in terms of how class, gender, and race dynamics figure in the arena of education policy.

In so doing, I treat these social categories as an integral part of the dominant cultural practices and political discourses in education, instead of something that operates in another realm. It is especially important to see these forces as mutually constitutive because the nature of education reforms has historically been inextricably bound up with teaching as a female-dominated profession (Apple, 1986). Moreover, I contend that recognizing this linkage allows for a more robust understanding of the forces animating the teachers' movement throughout the country at the current historical juncture. As discussed in previous chapters, one effect of neoliberal reforms in education has been to shift the discourse on education to one of evaluating teachers based on student progress as narrowly defined by standardized test results. The significance of this reform process for the purposes of this chapter is that "it is the history of the state, in concert with capital and a largely male academic body of consultants and developers, intervening at the level of practice into the work of a largely female workforce" (Apple, 1986, pp. 36–37). Meanwhile, reforms that effectively harm teachers in terms of their overall class position are almost always more severe in areas with a larger Black population.

In synthesizing critical feminist theory with the history of education reform initiatives and how they have disproportionately impacted Black majority students and educators, I advance five core arguments. Firstly, I argue that teachers generally reside at a contradictory class position— between the proletariat and petty bourgeoisie—though the pendulum tends to swing to the former in times of elite retrenchment, such as during the neoliberal epoch, with teachers especially singled out for "proletarianizing" reforms due to their gender profile.

Secondly, I engage with feminist scholarships to argue that teaching has historically been a gendered profession because of its position adjacent to other care work, i.e. reproductive labor, which has historically been viewed as uniquely befitting young women as they began to enter the workforce in the early to mid-twentieth century. Thirdly, I argue that teaching has historically been underpaid and singled out for monitorial management by paternalistic reformers, though female teachers have been able to push back more forcefully in recent years as they have gained leverage by being welcomed into other domains of work, and as teachers' unions have been established and gained strength throughout the country. Fourthly, I argue that feminized work—like teaching—is taking on increased importance in contemporary struggles because of the increasing centrality of immaterial labor in the social organization of leading economies.

Lastly, I discuss how race intersects with these class- and gender-based systems of discrimination and domination to further amplify neoliberal policies of retrenchment and control. I look at how fears of racial integration animated the early school reform movements, and how recent reforms have particularly focused on black and brown majority districts.

TEACHERS AS A CONTRADICTORY CLASS

Throughout this book, I have discussed the underlying movement dynamics largely in terms of control and autonomy of educators, and not so much in terms of class explicitly. The reason for this elision, thus far, is that teachers occupy a contradictory class position in society: existing between the "petty bourgeoisie" and the "working-class" (Apple, 1986; Wright, 1980). As such, the class dynamics are not as neatly bifurcated as they are in struggles in industrial workplaces between an ownership class that commands capital and a working-class commanded by capital. Moreover, education largely exists in the public domain, so that the vectors of control between ownership and workers are not as direct as it is in other workplaces.

Nonetheless, there are good reasons to discuss class as it pertains to struggles in the educational sector. First and foremost, the condition of teaching is quite often indicative of conditions in the broader workforce, and the struggles ongoing in the educational domain are reflective of struggles elsewhere. In this respect, the fate of teachers tacks with broader economic realities. While one could employ the "middle-class" moniker to describe the living conditions of teachers, that does not provide information on the relational characteristics of teachers in contemporary capitalist society. For the purposes of this project, it is far more instructive to inspect their contradictory presence in terms of how they relate to other relevant members of society. On the one hand, teachers share features in common with the working-class, especially in lean times when education is placed on the chopping block and subjected to the type of reforms discussed in the opening chapters of this book. On the other hand, teachers occupy what Wright (1980) refers to as a "semi-autonomous" domain of employment wherein they are afforded "a lot of freedom as to how (they) do (their) work" and the ability to "make a lot of decisions on (their) own" (p. 185). In the surveys conducted in Wright's study, teachers also tended to self-identify as managers, given their supervision of pupils, though he understandably places them in a different category than other supervisors. In describing the contradictory role of teachers, Apple (1986) argues that teachers' class position alternates between the "petty bourgeoisie and the working-class" depending on broader economic realities. When tight fiscal crises put education on the chopping block, teachers are pushed in the direction of the working-class.

Education does not exist apart from the economic and political domains, but is, rather, a reflection of those domains, and, by extension, the forces and relations that animate them. In sum, I believe that the teachers' movements of the last decade allow us to glimpse broader societal conflicts. The reason for this is that education is reproductive. However, unlike other critical scholars, such as Althusser (1971), Bowles and Gintis (1976), and Bernstein (1990), I do not argue that education simply reproduces the ruling ideology. Rather, I endorse the view of Apple (1986, 1995), Gramsci (1971), and Carnoy and Levin (1985) that education "is the product of conflict between the dominant and the dominated" (Carnoy & Levin, 1985). In other words, education is one of the key arenas in which a hegemonic compromise equilibrium is reached, and, as such, it embodies the tensions and contradictions present in society as a whole, while also being a place where new tensions emerge. To illustrate, the proletarianization of teachers in the neoliberal era has accompanied policies of rationalization that have effectively harmed and displaced working-class people in the United States. Traditional public schools constitute an important institution promoting social mobility and stability for working-class individuals. Policies designed to undermine that institution constitute an attack on proletarian communities.

THE ORIGIN OF CAPITALIST PATRIARCHY

Critical education scholars have noted that the gender dynamics of the teaching profession have made it easier to enact these disciplinary reforms. Socialist feminists have been particularly active in identifying a gendered division of labor in education, as part of a broader oeuvre that emerged out of a desire by women in the socialist movement to incorporate the gains made by the feminist tradition in the post-war era (Vogel, 2013). Their belief was that one could not adequately address class-based forms of oppression without also understanding the different roles assigned to the genders in capitalist society. The early inspiration for this scholarly intervention came from Engels' *The Origin of the Family, Private Property and the State*, wherein he locates the advent of patrilineal kinship groups in the rise of private property and early capitalist social relations. In a famous passage on this topic, he says:

> According to the materialistic conception, the determining factor in history is, in the final instance, the production and reproduction of immediate life. This, again, is of a twofold character: on the one side, the production of the means of existence, of food, clothing and shelter and the tools necessary for that production; on the other side, the production of human beings themselves, the propagation of the species. The social organization under which the people of a particular historical epoch and a particular country live is determined by both kinds of production: by the stage of development of labor on the one hand and of the family on the other (pp. 71–72).

Engels argues that with the rise of private property, men became the sole possessors of wealth, which he sees as a determining factor in the subjugation of women. He predicted that this subjugation would diminish as a result of women being drawn into wage labor as capitalism progressed. Vogel (2013) rejects this outlook as being too optimistic, as it negates the manner in which male dominance is constituted within proletarian households, and "vastly underestimates the variety of ideological and psychological factors that provide a continuing foundation for male supremacy in the working-class family" (Vogel, pp. 88–89).

However, Vogel's criticism of Engels is probably a bit harsh. *The Origin* did not seek to document every form of female subjugation that has ever existed, but, rather, to locate the material basis for sexism in the privileged place that men assumed with the rise of private property. His contribution to the understanding of the women's role in contemporary society is the recognition of the bifurcation between a male-dominated productive realm of work and a feminized reproductive domain that goes largely uncompensated.

Embedded in the bifurcation between productive and reproductive work lies a corresponding one between exchange-value and use-value: the former of which carries formal value in capitalist relations while the latter is largely uncompensated. Consigning women disproportionately to the realm of use-value, thus, has the effect of rendering them dependent on male workers operating in the productive economy. Women labor on behalf of male workers: both in terms of reproducing the "laboring body and the laboring subject" (Jarrett, 2016, p. 3).

Thus, rather than seeing the subjugation of women as unique to capitalism, Marxist feminists, instead, view a particular form of subjugation arising under capitalism, which is the relegation of women to an un- and under-paid function in the generation of capitalist social relations.

Federici (2004) argues that the root cause of this gendered division of labor was the land enclosures running between the sixteenth and eighteenth centuries. She holds that the commons, a reproductive site for small-scale agricultural producers, were also a place where women could be independent and socialize. While they still had a power disadvantage vis-à-vis men in earlier times, this was "tempered by the fact that they had access to the commons... while in the new capitalist regime women themselves became the commons, as their work was defined as a natural resource, laying outside the sphere of market relations" (Federici, 2004, p. 97).

Existing outside of the realm of the market, however, does not mean that domestic work is not essential to the functioning of capitalism. For one, it frees the male worker from domestic duties, in order that he can sell his labor power, which some scholars argue is tantamount to the generation of commodity value in its own right, as it allows man "to earn enough for a woman to reproduce him as labor power" (Dalla Costa & James, 1975, p. 34). Fortunati (1995) goes even further, arguing that reproductive work is, in fact, productive, because not only does it produce labor power, but it also generates surplus-value (though not in exchange-value form). However, in contradistinction, Vogel (2013) argues that it is better to think in terms of domestic labor as producing use-value. Her intervention is to instead situate domestic labor within the broader category of necessary labor, arguing that Marx neglected the domestic component thereof. Her rationale is that domestic labor allows the commodities purchased by a man's wage to be used: in the form of preparing raw food items for as a meal, for example.

Regardless of whether one situates domestic labor in the realm of use-value or in the commodity-producing realm of labor power, the commonality is in seeing domestic work as essential for the proper functioning of capitalism. As Jarrett (2016) notes, the family is part of the capitalist superstructure alongside education and other cultural institutions that serve to legitimate and naturalize existing social relations. She contends that capitalism has always needed certain conditions satisfied in order to function: a society that has subjects ready and willing to work where they are needed. In discussing how gender relations figure in the process of satisfying these conditions, Vogel (2013) explains that "they entail men's greater responsibility for provision of material means of subsistence, women's greater responsibility for the ongoing tasks of necessary labor, and institutionalized forms of male domination over women. While exceptions exist... the historical legacy remains one that has been characterized, for better or worse, as patriarchal." (pp. 154–155).

Nonetheless, the advantage that men have traditionally held through their dominance of productive work is not absolute. Fortunati (1995) notes that there is a humanizing element to reproductive work, which she argues serves to compensate for the alienating and dehumanizing nature of productive work. The sociality of home life gives workers the illusion that they are more than their labor power, i.e. their commodity form. Meanwhile, she notes that women have increasingly entered the productive realm in recent decades, which has resulted in them devoting less of their time to housework while increasingly paying others to fill in: something of a defeat for capitalists. Nonetheless, women still spend over two hours more per day on domestic work than men (Jarrett, 2016). As such, the entry into the productive workforce has not broken the chains disproportionately connecting women to reproductive work, though the shift has most certainly had implications on the stability of the gendered division of labor as a mechanism of control and legitimation of the existing social order.

At the same time, it is worth noting that a shift in the other direction has occurred, with men increasingly working in the immaterial economy. Autonomist Marxists have especially stressed this point. As mentioned in the last chapter, they have advanced the notion of the "social factory" to describe the contemporary nature of contentious politics not being confined to the workplace (Fortunati, 2007; Hardt & Negri, 2000, 2004; Jarret, 2016). They argue that this process is informed by the ever-increasing complexity of the workforce in a globalized economy, which expands the need for myriad service workers and specialists to coordinate business functions across international boundaries (Fortunati, 2007; Hardt & Negri, 2000, 2004). While traditional productive work has not vanished, autonomists argue that there has been a qualitative shift in labor toward the immaterial realm, which is to say that the leading edge of social relations and their attendant contradictions have moved in that direction (Dyer-Witheford, 1999; Hardt & Negri, 2000, 2004).

I take the autonomists' argument one step further by contending that the rise in the significance of immaterial labor has concomitantly served to heighten the importance of the educational realm—and other feminized domains of work—as a central site of contestation. First and foremost, this is because neoliberal reformers have traditionally singled out education as a place for attacks. As Apple (1986, 1995) underscores, and as I mentioned in the previous chapters, neoliberal governance routinely exports blame for economic and social problems to the educational realm. This tendency has, in turn, been the impetus for the reforms that have played a large role in provoking the teachers' movements that are the focus of this study. Moreover, those reforms have mobilized patriarchal logics that see teaching as a logical target because of the largely female workforce in place.

Professional Autonomy and its Contradictions

The large-scale entry of women into the teaching workforce in the United States and other western countries began in earnest during the mid-nineteenth century, owing to a composite of economic and cultural factors. As far as economic forces go, there were both demand-side and supply-side forces pulling women into the profession. In the former case, rapid population expansion during this period coupled with the growth of a public commitment to universal education created an explosion in teaching opportunities. Meanwhile, on the supply side, this period was marked by the rapid expansion in the education of young women, giving them the requisite qualifications in a period where the profession came under increasing standardization (a factor that led to teaching being less attractive to many men at the time) (Apple, 1986; Strober &

Tyack, 1980). At the same time, women were categorically excluded from working in other professional domains at the time, such as business and commerce: domains that men were then entering in large numbers (Strober & Tyack, 1980).

Meanwhile, teaching work was seen as consistent with the Victorian cult of domesticity that defined women's lives in that era. It was not too distant a departure from housework to teaching in the eyes of those advocating the femininization of the profession, including reformers like Catharine Beecher and Horace Mann, who argued that the nurturing skills that made women good mothers would transfer well to education (Strober & Tyack, 1980; Vaughn-Roberson, 1992). Strober and Tyack (1980) summarize this sentiment as also offering an opportunity for upper-class women to not degrade themselves in the way that toiling in a factory would: "To women from families of higher status, teaching was one of the few occupations widely distributed geographically and acceptable for respectable young women" (p. 496). The prevailing ethos of the time also held that teaching kept with women's altruistic tendencies more than other paid work, which "degraded women and corrupted their moral character" (Carter, 1990, p. 124). Catharine Beecher (1846, as cited in Carter, 1990) embodied this sentiment in her entreaty calling for "Christian females" to work "not for money, nor influence, nor for honor, not for ease, but with the simple, single purpose of doing good" (p. 23).

The practical effect of these calls to enter the profession on altruistic ground was to place downward pressure on the wages of female teachers, given that teachers were supposed to be motivated by a sense of service to God and community, not their financial compensation (Carter, 1990). As a result, women were paid substantially less than their male counterparts until the early twentieth century. Despite calls for equal wages, school boards of the era were reluctant to approve the significant spending hikes that would be necessary to eliminate the pay gap. Meanwhile, they were averse to cutting male teacher wages because men could always find better paying jobs elsewhere, and they were seen as playing a valuable role as role models for male students and as disciplinarians and administrators (Carter, 1990). Nonetheless, the low wages ultimately stoked contradictions, as many women struggled to realize the image of bourgeois femininity animating the domestic ideal of that era, which ultimately led to the departure from the profession of many women from wealthier families, especially as opportunities began to open elsewhere in the early twentieth century (Carter, 1990).

Nonetheless, a gendered division of labor in education persists to this day. While the pay disparity between genders is smaller than it once was, men are still disproportionately represented the higher one goes in the educational hierarchy, especially at the level of district leadership (Apple & Jungck, 1990; Superville, 2016). In this regard, Superville (2016) notes that women make up 76% of teachers while accounting for less than a quarter of all superintendents in this country.

As referenced earlier, the dynamic that emerges out of this division of labor is one of male managers implementing top-down reforms upon a female-dominated workforce (Apple, 1986; Altenbaugh, 1990). Moreover, teaching has always been singled out for administrative oversight and Taylorist mechanisms of control. As part of the zeitgeist of scientific management and efficiency in the early twentieth century, school systems developed district bureaucracies to micromanage their school systems, which had the net effect of reducing the decision-making role of teachers in the educational process, on the one hand, while also reducing education policy largely to questions of cost, with an emphasis on keeping teacher wages low (Altenbaugh, 1990). As neo-Taylorist policies were applied under the rubric of neoliberalism, these mechanisms have become more exhaustive, and the stakes have gotten higher.

However, Apple (1986) notes that, in the earlier days of these bureaucratic interventions from above, many teachers saw the reforms as helping professionalize their work. The standardization and rationalization accompanying outside reforms were often perceived as factors contributing to the legitimation of their work. This response is especially understandable when one considers that women have traditionally been situated in workplaces more susceptible to proletarianization, including housework, clerical work, and other service work, which has resulted in a tendency to embrace professionalism as a defense mechanism (Apple, 1986). Thus, a contradiction emerges between autonomy and professionalism in the lives of women workers. The reforms injecting greater professional standards (or at least the appearance thereof) into their work tend to come in the form of a patriarchal hierarchy: male reformers and administrators dictating the working lives of the female majority teaching corps. Many women, eager to be accepted as legitimate members of the professional workforce, embraced the reforms despite the larger paternalistic social structure around them.

That said, there was never a time where all teachers passively accepted the dictates from above. Altenbaugh (1990) notes: "A few resisted, many acquiesced, and others collectively asserted themselves" (p. 169). As teachers' unions were established through the course of the early twentieth century, the numbers of those resisting began steadily increasing. Fittingly for the purposes of this project, one of the first noteworthy voices of militant resistance emerged out of Chicago in the form of Margaret Haley, a representative with the Chicago Teachers' Federation and subsequent co-founder of the American Federation of Teachers (AFT). At the 1904 gathering of the National Education Association (NEA), she condemned "factory-izing education," and drew linkages between the treatment faced by teachers and that experienced by those working in manual labor positions (Carter, 1990). In addressing the top-down control instituted on teaching, she declared, "The individuality of the teacher and her power of initiative are thus destroyed and the result is courses of study, regulations, and equipment which the teachers have had no voice in selecting, which often have no relation to the children's needs, and which prove a hindrance instead of a help in teaching" (Haley, p. 216).

For her, these interventions failed to provide for what she saw as the principal objective of the education system: "to preserve and develop the democratic ideal" (Carter, 1990). She was effectively presaging the battle lines that would become ever more vivid a century later: the gulf between an instrumentalist, rationalizing view of education on the one hand, and the altruistic view on the other hand, with its emphasis on education as a mechanism for cultivating a robust citizenry. At the same time, she represented perhaps the most radical example of the break that had occurred with the Victorian cult of domesticity that reigned over the teaching profession over much of the previous half century. While she retained the altruistic notion that her work as serving a vital social function, she rejected the notion that this function could be delivered absent a workforce operating with autonomy and dignity.

Meanwhile, among the more politically moderate and conservative sectors of the profession, the mindset shifted from that of "altruistic social servant to the socially-conscious but fiscally-concerned worker" (Carter, 1990, p. 136). As opportunities slowly began to open elsewhere for women, they began considering the economic implications of teaching work for themselves and their family and began weighing that consideration against the altruistic call to duty (Carter, 1990). They now behaved far more like their male counterparts engaged in manual labor: bargaining for better conditions, making demands of their employers and lawmakers, and demonstrating willingness to leave for greener pastures elsewhere when possible.

Women were originally drawn into the profession via a cult of domesticity that emphasized the altruistic mission of the métier: a logic that would transfer to subsequent movements within the teaching rank via an embrace of the notion that education serves a higher purpose in society than reformers allow with their "factory-ization" of schools.

The early noises of protest by the likes of Margaret Haley presaged what would come over a century later, with a still-majority female teaching corps facing off against neo-Taylorist mechanisms of management and control promulgated as part of the neoliberal offensive of the last 50 years.

Race and Racism in the Battle for the Soul of Education

Race and class are inextricably linked in American history, as the former has always been used as justification, legitimation, and amplification for a class-based society. Race is a social construct that is born of class-based societies to provide a subaltern segment of society that is subjected to the most extreme forms of exploitation, and whose very presence keeps lower-class whites in line by providing an "other" over whom they can feel a sense of superiority. Race serves the interest of the ruling elite, because it is easier to justify policy that exploits the working-class when there are racialized strata thereof, with Black populations being harmed and marginalized more than their white counterparts.

One can rather clearly glimpse this tendency with regard to recent neoliberal education reforms, which were pressed most aggressively in Black majority districts, most notably in Chicago and New Orleans. As discussed earlier, Chicago became a laboratory for neoliberal education reforms starting in the closing decades of the twentieth century and accelerating in the early twenty-first century. In 2013, then-Mayor Rahm Emanuel slated 53 schools for closure to help close a nearly $1 billion deficit on the grounds that they were failing to meet standards loosely based on Obama's *Race to the Top* legislation. Of those schools, 91% had a majority Black student body, and 72% also had a majority Black teaching corps, despite only about 30% of Chicago Public School teachers as a whole being African American (Chicago Teachers' Union, 2013).

But nowhere was the neoliberal overhaul of education more thoroughgoing than in post-Katrina New Orleans. Reformers there had the benefit of a natural disaster that visited unprecedented devastation upon the city when Katrina made landfall on the Louisiana in 2005. Much of the school infrastructure was damaged or completely destroyed by the flooding that followed the failure of the city's main levee system, necessitating that serious investment be made to rehabilitate the system. But rather than rebuild the existing public school stock, reformers seized on the opportunity to engage in what Naomi Klein (2007) calls disaster capitalism, when natural disasters are exploited as opportunity to jam through radical neoliberal privatization schemes while a location is in the disarray that prevails in a storm's wake. University of Chicago Economics School champion Milton Friedman called on the city to turn to voucher programs to fill the void left by the disaster, and dozens of think tanks heeded his call and swooped in to fund such initiatives. Meanwhile, the second Bush administration provided hundreds of millions of dollars for the construction of new alternative charter schools. When all was said and done, New Orleans only had four traditional public schools remaining out of an original count of 123. All 4,700 members of the city's teachers' union had been fired: 71% of which were Black and 78% of which were women (Klein, 2007).

It is no accident that this market fundamentalism was ultimately enacted in a city like New Orleans. Voucher programs, in particular, were first devised as a scheme by which white families could evade desegregation laws in the south. The programs were concocted by James Buchanan and G. Warren Nutter as a mechanism to technically embrace desegregation while effectively keeping schools segregated in 1970s Virginia (Maclean, 2017). Whites could use the vouchers to send their kids to privately run schools away from the communities being forced to integrate, all under the rubric of "school choice." Meanwhile, the market fundamentalists, including Milton Friedman, gladly embraced the measures for its promise of choice and flexibility: two neoliberal mantras.

But the racist nature of education reforms does not end with voucher programs and school closures in predominantly black areas. In recent years, white supremacist policymakers have specifically targeted school curricula for being too "woke" in its treatment of race and racism with a litany of bills passed in various states, counties, and municipalities throughout the country. These laws have attempted to muzzle educators from addressing the country's history of structural racism by prohibiting pedagogical practices loosely lumped together under the moniker "critical race theory."

Struggles Both Old and New

Class, race, and gender are bound up with one another when it comes to the treatment of educators, in much the same way that economic structure bears on cultural practice more generally. In order to understand the tendency of teachers to be proletarianized during times of cutbacks in public services, one must also understand the gendered division of labor that has historically existed in capitalist societies wherein women have been disproportionately relegated to the un- and undercompensated sector of care work. The subsequent entry of women into teaching work has always been characterized by conflict between the feminized teaching corps and the majority-male managers in administration and leadership (Apple, 1986). The practices of discrimination and marginalization present in the cultural arena and the forces of domination and control that prevail in the economic domain are commingled in the educational domain. Understanding education's political battles necessitates an appreciation of both sides to this social dynamic.

Not only does the current wave of teachers' movement emerge out of the crisis of neoliberal capitalism, but it also descends from over a century of cultural struggle of women workers entering the workforce and fighting for dignity and autonomy in their professional lives. As women have entered other professional domains at the same time, they have gained more leverage with which to bargain, at the same time that the proliferation of teachers' unions throughout the country has given them institutional strength with which to wage their battles. Nonetheless, recent reforms severely curtailing the right of these unions to collectively bargain and stripping teachers of hard-won autonomy have set teachers back in terms of many of the gains they made in the early part of the twentieth century, effectively opening old wounds in the educational domain.

The opening of these wounds is one of the principal factors motivating the teachers' movement of the last decade. However, I also contend that another significant factor is that education has become a more important cultural institution in an age where immaterial labor has become ever more central in the social organization of countries in the economic core.

The locus of struggle has, likewise, shifted in a decidedly immaterial direction, with teachers taking center stage. Much of the focus of neoliberal reforms has been on control and management of people and message: of injecting market discipline into the psyche of the nation while legitimating that discipline through the dominant logics circulating in the cultural terrain. Education has been singled out as a domain in which to activate the evaluative and monitorial mechanisms of control precisely because of its obvious importance in the battle over ideas. It is, thus, little surprise that it has also become one of the central sites of political struggle at a time when neoliberalism's guiding logics have fallen into crisis.

References

Altenbaugh, R. (1990). Teachers and the workplace. In R. J. Altenbaugh (Ed.), *The teachers's voice: A social history of teaching in twentieth century America* (pp. 124–136).

Althusser, L. (1971/2014). *On the reproduction of capitalism: Ideology and ideological state apparatuses.* Verso.

Apple, M., & Jungck, S. (1990). "You don't have to be a teacher to teach this unit": Teaching, technology and gender in the classroom. *American Educational Research Journal, 27*(2), 227–251.

Apple, M. (1986). *Teachers and texts: A political economy of class and gender relations in education.* Routledge.

Apple, M. (1995). *Education and power* (2nd ed.). Routledge.

Bernstein, B. (1990). *The Structuring of Pedagogic Discourse.* Routledge.

Bowles, S., & Gintis, H. (1976). *Schooling in capitalist America: Educational reform and the contradictions of economic life.* Basic Books.

Carnoy, M., & Levin, H. (1985). *Schooling and work in the democratic state.* Stanford University Press.

Carter, P. (1990). The social status of women teachers in the early twentieth century. In R. J. Altenbaugh (Ed.), *The teachers's voice: A social history of teaching in twentieth century America* (pp. 124–136).

Chicago Teachers' Union (2013, April 18). Disproportionate number of teacher layoffs are black and latino. [Press release]. https://www.ctulocal1.org/posts/school-closuresfacts-and-statistics/.

Dalla Costa, M., & James, S. (1975). *The power of women and the subversion of the community.* Falling Wall Press.

Dyer-Witheford, N. (1999). *Cyber-Marx: Cycles and circuits of struggle in high-technology capitalism.* University of Illinois Press.

Federici, S. (2004). *Caliban and the witch.* Autonomedia.

Fortunati, L. (1995). *The arcane of reproduction: Housework, prostitution, labor and capital.* Autonomedia.
Fortunati, L. (2007). Immaterial labor and its machinization. *Ephemera, 7*(1), 139–157.
Gramsci, A. (1971). In Q. Hoare, & G. Nowell-Smith (Eds.), *Selections from the prison notebooks of Antonio Gramsci.* International Publishers.
Hardt, M., & Negri, A. (2000). *Empire.* Harvard University Press.
Hardt, M., & Negri, A. (2004). *Multitude: War and democracy in the age of Empire.* The Penguin Press.
Jarrett, K. (2016). *Feminism, labour and digital media.* Routledge.
Klein, N. (2007). *The shock doctrine: The rise of disaster capitalism.* Picador.
MacLean, N. (2017). *Democracy in chains: The deep history of the radical right's stealth plan for America.* Penguin.
Strober, M., & Tyack, D. (1980). Why do women teach and men manage? A report on research in school. *Signs, 5*(3), 494–503.
Superville, D. (2016, November 15). Few women run the nation's school districts. Why? *Education Week.* Retrieved from, www.edweek.org
Vaughn-Roberson, C. (1992). Having a purpose in life: Western women teachers in the twentieth century. In R. J. Altenbaugh (Ed.), *The Teachers's Voice*, A social history of teaching in twentieth century America (pp. 12–24).
Vogel, L. (1983/2013). *Marxism and the oppression of women: Toward a unitary theory* (Rev. ed.). Haymarket Books.
Wright, E. O. (1980). Class and Occupation. *Theory and Society, 9*(1), 177–214.

CHAPTER 5

Teachers in the Circuits of Communication

Abstract This chapter provides a model for how discourses about education flow through different sectors of society in providing the basis for education policy and then legitimating that policy. In developing this model, I look back at history of neoliberal reforms discussed in Chapter 3 and show how these reforms were justified using rhetoric about a "crisis in education." That crisis rhetoric was deployed to explain the flagging economy of the early 1980s, as well as the perception that the United States was losing ground to countries like Germany and Japan in terms of competitive dynamism in automotive and computer technology. In essence, an economic crisis was discursively displaced to the educational realm, with teachers being disproportionately blamed for the country's waning competitive edge: a discourse that was then employed in legitimating reforms designed to disproportionately hold teachers accountable for student performance.

Keywords Reagan education policy · Crisis in education · Neoliberal education reforms · Education discourses · Crisis of stagflation · Media portrayals of teachers · Media portrayals of education

In Chapter 3, I delineated the historical forces that gave rise to neoliberalism as a governing project, and how neoliberal logics have been applied

© The Author(s), under exclusive license to Springer Nature Switzerland AG 2025
M. Reichel, *Teacher Power in the Digital Age*, Social Movements and Transformation, https://doi.org/10.1007/978-3-031-87191-7_5

within the domain of education broadly. I specifically highlighted the case of Chicago because it was used as something of a laboratory for neoliberal education reforms, on the one hand, but also because I argue that the CTU has been central as a catalyst for broader sectoral change in the organizational structures and communicative dynamics of teacher unions that has continued with the rolling walkouts of 2018–19.

This chapter turns the focus to the flow of education discourses through society in order to emphasize the importance of teacher activists' communicative and discursive interventions. Because so much of the neoliberal offensive on education was built upon cultivating an image of teachers and school as inept and dysfunctional in communicative circuits—e.g. the news media, the realm of political discourses as well as the entertainment media—it has been especially important for teachers to counter that portrayal with an image of their own. In other words, it has not been enough for teachers to engage in traditional bargaining around contractual issues because so much of the neoliberal reform process has been justified with political rhetoric about education being in crisis and, thus, in need of a dose of market discipline. At the same time, the entertainment and news media have both tended to portray teachers as a central part of the problem, treating them variously as inept, lazy, out-of-touch, and conservative in their worldview (Ayers, 2001; Goldstein, 2011; Kantor et al, 2001). The image that emerges is one of an antiquated institution in desperate need of market discipline in order to bring it into line with the needs of contemporary society.

There has been significant work done on news media framing as both justifying and naturalizing the reforms comporting with the neoliberal counteroffensive of this era (Apple 2001, 2013; Berliner & Biddle, 1995; Goldstein, , 2014; Goldstein, 2011; Lipman, 2011). Meanwhile, others have inspected the role of pop culture films and television shows in furthering the image of educational crisis and the need for savior teachers to swoop in and save the inept mass of teachers (Ayers, 2001; Kantor et al, 2001).

Nonetheless, there is little in the way of theory with which to situate these discourses within broader economic and political power structures as logics of legitimation. Moreover, this is an important hole to fill, given the centrality of educational practice in the formation and transmission of dominant logics, and the creation of space from which to interrogate those structures (Apple 2013; Bernstein, 1990). As such, this chapter holds that media framing of education is inherently different than most instances of framing, because it involves the portrayal of an institution that serves a similar role to the mass media itself: one involved in meaning-making and the promulgation of narrative and discourse (Gitlin, 2003; Thomas, 2011).

In this chapter, I develop a heuristic model to chart the flow of discourses through societal circuits: the political arena, the news and entertainment media, the realm of educational practice, and within the teachers' movement (as a counterhegemonic discursive intervention). The objective with this heuristic is to illuminate how logics embedded in discourses are naturalized via their re-contextualization across different societal spaces. At the same time, it is important to note that no discourses flow in a closed system. While the elite have an advantage in setting the bounds of discourse, this is never complete. Teachers, due to their occupation of a critical chokepoint in the circulation of discourses, have the power to contest them as part of their counterhegemonic communicative intervention. Because schoolteachers, especially in the public sector, constitute one of the few professions that remains heavily unionized in this country and elsewhere, they are particularly well-positioned to challenge policy that they deem detrimental to a healthy educational environment, in addition to the logics and media frames deployed to justify those policies.

This capacity for contestation not only comes through union activity, but also via the quotidian interactions that teachers have with students and community members. Owing to the amount of time that teachers spend with pupils, they are some of the few figures outside of the household that can compete with the mass media in structuring the ways in which young people perceive the world (Apple, 1995, 2013). While curricula tend to reflect culturally hegemonic views, their enactment is a contested process with room for resistance. In other words, economic structure does not determine educational practice, but rather conditions the contradictory process of production and reproduction of knowledge (Apple, 1995).

Education is also a site of community struggle, as evinced in the prominent part that schools have historically played in the racial justice movement in this country's history. Apple (2013) notes: "Struggles over schooling—over what should be taught, over the relationship between schools and local communities, over the very ends and means of the institution itself—have provided a crucible for the formation of larger social movements toward equality" (p. 20). In this sense, teachers are not passive subjects upon whom dominant discourses are brought to bear: they are actively engaged in an interdiscursive relationship with the power elite and mass media, through their pedagogical interventions and community activism.

This chapter aims to inspect the nature of this interdiscursivity, by addressing the question of how the mass media treatment of teachers relates to larger structural forces that inform the onset of neoliberalism as a governing logic. Given the preponderance of "crisis" talk within media framing of education, how do economic and social crises bear on discourses surrounding the form and function of education in society? What has been the effect of teachers' contestation of this crisis narrative, and how have they been able to transform the larger discourse more to their favor? Lastly, what model emerges of the relationship between teachers and the mass media in the ongoing conversation about the role of education in society?

These questions will be addressed in three steps, each with its own dedicated section. Firstly, I will flesh out a theoretical framework that relates educational policy and practice via the interdiscursive struggle between policymakers and teachers. This section will distill literature arguing that education practice emerges from dominant, but contested, discourses that get re-contextualized in subsequent stages of campaign rhetoric, policy enactment, pedagogical practice, and popular discourse on education.

Secondly, I will delineate the mass media's role in this cycle, by showing how an "education in crisis" trope emerged from pop culture and reappeared in news media coverage of education policy and teachers. In addition to highlighting some of the manifestations of mass media framing, this section will use Iyengar's (1991) typology to argue that the tendency has been to cover education policy thematically (as being in "crisis"), while covering teachers episodically (as alternatively being responsible for the crisis or being the outside savior that swoops in to save the dysfunctional system).

Thirdly, this crisis talk will be framed as reflecting a broader economic and social malaise that emerged out of the economic stagnation of the 1970s. In this vein, I concede that there is a crisis of sorts, but that it is rooted in broad economic and social structures, which, nonetheless, bear on the educational realm because of the latter's central role in the formation and transmission of logics of legitimation of these dominant structures. In concluding, I will argue that media framing of education is part of a broader interdiscursive process of structuring the dominant social and political order, addressing its problems, and attempting to resolve its internal crises.

EDUCATION AND THE INTERDISCURSIVE STRUGGLE OVER POLICY FRAMES

I hold that the study of the mass media framing of education is not analogous to other framing studies, because of the unique role that education plays in the production of dominant logics alongside the mass media itself. As Gitlin (2003) relates: "It is the cultural industry as a whole, along with the educational system, that most coherently specializes in the production, relaying, and regearing of hegemonic ideology" (p. 254).

While it is probably always overly simplistic to see framing as a unidirectional process, it would be particularly problematic in media coverage of education. Therefore, it is important to flesh out a theoretical framework showing how educational practice and policy formations are commingled in an interdiscursive cycle.

In doing so, I will build on three core assumptions about the function of education in society taken from radical pedagogy. Firstly, ideological discourses occurring in society writ large are mirrored in the realm of education through struggle over policy and structure. In other words, political rhetoric and education practice share an intertwined relationship through which knowledge and policy are created and transferred (Bernstein, 1990). Secondly, education is the central terrain wherein debates over what constitutes knowledge are carried out, and, by extension, status is distributed (Apple, 1995; Bowles and Gintis, 1976). Thirdly, this process is contested, thus rendering the educational realm inherently contradictory, insofar as it serves to legitimate existing power relations while also privileging diversity and openness in a way that often threatens entrenched power (Apple, 1995; Bernstein, 1990; Bowles & Gintis, 1976). In this sense, education is involved in both production and reproduction, and, thus, serves both an economic and cultural function. In other words, it is not just a site of the distribution of knowledge and status, but also a site wherein cultural hegemony is established in a contested and contradictory process (Apple, 1995). Taken together, these assumptions reveal education to be a terrain of struggle over politics and identity: one that reflects broader processes of "coming to be" in a democratic society characterized by ever-evolving conflict about the purpose and direction of that society.

Bernstein (1990) provides a model for how ideological discourses are transferred from society writ large to the educational realm. He sees this process as occurring on the three fronts of production, reproduction, and re-contextualization. These correspond, respectively, to the development of new knowledge, the transmission of knowledge through pedagogical practice, and the field where discourses and logics around production are transferred into different contexts (Bernstein, 1990). By mediating the process of the development and dissemination of knowledge in addition to the larger conversation around the nature and function of schooling, educators occupy a parallel and comingled arena with the political arena in which dominant discourses are constructed and transmitted. Moreover, these discourses are transferred from context to context in a manner that naturalizes their underlying assumptions (Apple 2001, Bernstein, 1990).

Regarding the transfer of neoliberal logics into the educational realm, Apple (2001) charts how the neoliberal consensus emerged as a marriage of convenience of several different political strands. He emphasizes that there was no grand conspiracy of sorts behind the push for market reforms, but rather a confluence of forces:

> An economic context in which public spending was under severe scrutiny and cost savings had to be sought everywhere; government officials who were opposed to "frills" and consistently intervened to institute only a selection of the recommendations; ideological attacks on critical, progressive, or child-centered approaches to physical education; and a predominant discourse on "being pragmatic" (p. 75).

Support for these reforms came, in part, from a technical and managerial middle class, not out of ideological resonance, per se, but because of the fact they possessed the expertise necessary for implementation of an education agenda built around "ideologies of control measurement and efficiency" (Apple, 2001, p. 48). As such, their economic security and class mobility hinged on the capacity to provide the technical services necessary to enact the regimes of testing and evaluation that serve to sort the population by class in the neoliberal era. Apple (2001) also notes that the broader middle class tends to possess the necessary "cultural capital" to negotiate the increasingly complex and multifarious admissions regimes that have emerged in the heavily "charterized" education landscape. Moreover, many members of minority communities have embraced these reforms for affording them the opportunity to be treated as consumers in a system that had previously closed them off in an eviscerated public sector. Meanwhile, those possessing the cultural capital necessary to navigate the admissions procedures of selective charter schools have occasionally realized appreciable gains in education quality for their children (Apple, 2001; Lipman, 2011).

In sum, a particular set of logics regarding education practice was naturalized in the policy formation process and then embraced by large segments of the population that could benefit economically. These logics grew out of a discourse on education quality that framed a supposed crisis as emerging, and largely attributed that crisis to teacher performance, as mentioned in the last chapter with regard to the Reagan administration's stemming from its publication of "A Nation at Risk" (Goldstein, 2014). The reports used alarmist language about the country's flagging economic competitiveness, while transferring blame for these economic woes squarely on the shoulders of teachers, lamenting that: "Too many teachers are being drawn from the bottom quarter of graduating high school and college students." It does not indicate how many are taken from the bottom quarter, or what a desirable benchmark would be. Moreover, it does not bother to contextualize this statistic, by showing, for example, the differences between suburban and inner-city schools, nor does it interrogate the race and class-based divisions in education quality, and the deep-seated structural biases that explain these divisions.

The report abstracts its assessment of schools from social and economic structure, while invoking a moral panic about the direction of the country (Goldstein, 2014). While many of its recommendations are reasonable, such as the longer school day, the administration ultimately focused its attention on cost-cutting measures, as part of its larger orientation on lean government. Meanwhile, the Democratic Party, which had previously been willing to defend teachers and public schools, found itself having to compromise on a lot of these issues, owing to an implosion of popular support for public education (Goldstein, 2014). The Reagan administration had effectively set the discursive agenda with its crisis narrative, which became naturalized in the public's eyes as it cycled through enacted policy and into broader societal discourse, ultimately devouring what was once the opposition party on social issues like these.

Eventually, teacher frustration with these reforms began to simmer over. In 2010, the Caucus of Rank-and-File Educators (CORE) won leadership of the Chicago Teachers' Union (CTU), and latterly went on strike in 2012 to contest the school closings and the larger problem of pedagogy rooted in standardized test results (Brogan, 2013; Lipman, 2011). While a recently passed state bill required the strike to be based on narrow contractual demands, they effectively toed a tenuous line in raising the broader critiques of the ongoing reform process and initiating a public discourse on the role of education in local communities (Brogan, 2013, 2014; Lipman, 2011; Uetricht, 2014). In CTU president Karen Lewis's words, the strike was about "the very soul of education" (Brogan, 2014).

With this, the CTU initiated a counter-discourse on the importance of local schools to the communities in which they are embedded (Brogan, 2013, 2014; Uetricht, 2014). The CTU was able to gain widespread public support for their efforts, despite the media campaign being lodged against them (Uetricht, 2014). In sum, the need to apply market discipline to schools has gone from dominant discourse to formal policy to naturalized logic, while an emerging counter-discourse has risen and already realized some success in upending the formal policy and its logic of legitimation.

Mass Media's Role: Naturalizing the Crisis Trope

Understanding the role of mass media in contributing to this interdiscursive cycle is vital, owing to the ubiquity and prominence of media in the current era (Kellner & Share, 2007). Moreover, many scholars have remarked on the symbiotic relationship between traditional mainstream news media and political elites in framing the political agenda (Bennett & Graber, 2007; Walgrave & Van Aelst, 2006), while also being able to generate consent around a set of dominant principles (Herman & Chomsky, 1988). Meanwhile, Delli Carpini and Williams (2001) note that the multiaxial nature of contemporary media permits entertainment media to influence political discourse as well. As such, this section considers depictions of education and educators across various media forms, looking for congruence of certain themes and narrative patterns, and then connecting these tendencies to the discourses outlined in the previous section.

The objective here is not to unearth an elite conspiracy operating within media organizations, but rather to use news coverage to highlight how the "primary definers,"—i.e. the institutional voices that the news and entertainment media amplify—tend to conceive of education, teachers, and their movements (Hall, 2013). In other words, I hold that the media is a useful referential source for understanding dominant viewpoints because of the sheer power that elite voices have in terms of being the principal sources for news coverage, while also being disproportionately responsible for the production and dissemination of content more generally. As Hall (2013) relates: "The media... do not simply... transmit the ideology of the 'ruling class'... but their structured relationship to power has the effect of making them play a crucial but secondary role in *reproducing* the definitions of those who have privileged access, as a right, to the media as "accredited sources" (p. 62). Hall's conceptualization mirrors Herman and Chomsky's (1988) sourcing filter, through which "the mass media are drawn into a symbiotic relationship with powerful sources of information by economic necessity and reciprocity of interest." A frame analysis, thus, permits one to glimpse power structures operating beneath the human practices being reported upon.

Moreover, I hold that the teachers' movements represent a privileged vantage point from which to glimpse the crisis of neoliberal hegemony and the concomitant efforts to forge a new hegemonic consensus, because education plays a central role in the social steering process. In this regard, Althusser (1971) assigns to education the role of the dominant "ideological state apparatus" (ISA) in advanced capitalist societies, owing to the sheer amount of time pupils spend under the watchful eye of school systems. While I endorse this view, I reject the functionalism at work in Althusser's formulation, whereby economic determinacy is recovered "in the last instance," so that the cultural institutions are only autonomous until the hard edge of structure has had its imprint.

Following Gramsci (1971) and Hall (2016), I look at structure as having a conditioning rather than determining effect. In discussing the tendencies and constraints that emerge from economic structure, Hall (2016) argues:

> The error of reductionism is then to translate these tendencies and constraints immediately into their absolutely determined political and ideological effects or, alternatively, to abstract them into some "iron law of necessity." In fact, they structure and determine only in the sense that they define the terrain on which historical forces move; they define the horizon of possibilities. But they can neither in the first nor last instance fully determine the content of political and economic struggles, much less objectively fix or guarantee the outcomes of such struggles. (p. 160)

I would further complicate Althusser's (1971) formulation by arguing that there is not just one dominant ISA in the current epoch. It seems clear that the mass media plays at least an equally significant role in contemporary society, effectively acting as a separate pole pulling at children in their formative years. However, the respective roles these institutions play in society are markedly different in their form and function. For one, education systems are more democratic in nature than the mass media, as there is simply more room for counterhegemonic voices: in the form of teachers' unions, the relative autonomy teachers have in pedagogical decisions (though this has arguably waned in recent years), and also the centrality of schools as sites for the organization of broader movements (Apple, 2013).

As such, I would contend that educational systems are more representative of the contradictions undergirding hegemonic crises like the current one. They are more adaptable and open to public pressures and draw upon a much larger percentage of the population, given that all children are required to spend their entire day at school every day. Meanwhile, the mass media tends to be more under elite control, with popular pressure limited to the consumptive end of the dissemination cycle.

Thus, while the mass media and educators do not exist in strict tension with one another, they are conditioned by sufficiently disparate forces to allow for some tensions to emerge. More fundamentally, I would argue that these tensions emerge out of the contradictions born of the interplay between ideology and social forces, which Hall (2016) describes as being dialectical in nature. In this formulation, a dominant ideology is promulgated and legitimated by major cultural institutions, including both mass media and education, but the underlying contradictions are witnessed within the school systems more so than within mass media, owing to the former's relative openness to forces outside of its own circle of legitimation. In the current case, neoliberal logics have spread through both institutions, but contradictions have spilled over in the educational realm due to the direct, adverse effect of these policies and practices on teachers, together with teachers' capacity to organize through unions (and otherwise), and to draw upon support in the community (Brogan, 2013, 2014; Lipman, 2011).

Furthermore, I hold that these contradictions are, in turn, animated by the tension between two different idealizations of the role of education in society. On one side is the traditional liberal, Deweyan view, which sees education as playing a prominent role in the cultivation of a robust and engaged citizenry; on the other side is the neoliberal view, which seeks to reduce education to a measurable instrumentality, as part of a broader process of market rationalization driving education policy (Lipman, 2011). While the latter view has been hegemonic for much of the last forty years, the former never vanished.

A Heuristic Model of Discursive Flows on Education

The model illustrated below is designed to show the flow of discourses between cultural arenas that are of concern to this study. As a heuristic, it is not meant to be totalistic in nature. Clearly, there are adjacent cultural spaces that absorb the flow of discourses, and these discourses are challenged at each step along the way and synthesized with other discourses, and so on. Nonetheless, once a discourse becomes dominant, as neoliberal rationalizations had become by about the 1980s, when they were popular in political and media spaces, and able to bear on educational discourses through the activity of zealous reformers, then they tend to flow from circuit to circuit relatively freely. The process of re-contextualization between political discourse, education policy, education practice, and popular discourse is marked by arrows following the flow clockwise. Meanwhile, I note that the two opposing poles of political discourse and educational practice are, respectively, dominated by the influence of mass media and teachers. The latter point is taken as a given, since teachers still tend to hold a great deal of autonomy in designing and enacting curriculum (even as some of this power is being taken away in this era of reform). Moreover, class time tends to be composed purely of interaction among students and between students and teachers, with minimal media influence. The realm of educational practice is one where teacher influence is dominant (Fig. 5.1).

Between these poles lie the intermediating realms of "education policy" and "popular discourse." The former emerges from processes of political deliberation on how to structure education systems, while the latter constitutes the variegated responses of individuals to their educational experience. While education policy is not dominated by mass media effects, it results from political discourses that are. Likewise, popular reaction to educational experience is colored by the effect of teachers on the lives of former pupils. Through day-to-day interactions with students, teachers transmit certain value-sets and mores that are separate from the

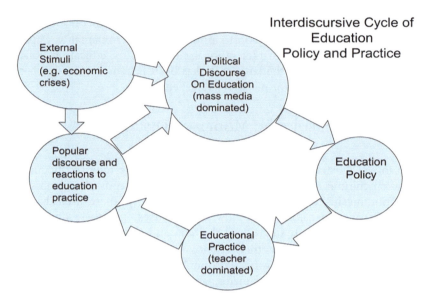

Fig. 5.1 Interdiscursive cycle of education and practice

formal curriculum, but that nonetheless play an important role in the development of pupils' understanding of the world around them (Apple, 1995, 2013). On this note, Apple (2013) relates:

> Children spend a very large part of their lives inside the buildings we call schools. They come to grips with authority relations, with the emotional labor both of managing one's presentation of self and of being with others who are both the same and different. Transformations in the content and structure of this key organization have lasting effects on the dispositions and values that we do and do not act upon, on who we think we are and on who we think we can become. Care, love, and solidarity—or the absence of them—are among the constitutive building blocks of one's identity. (p. 20)

Meanwhile, the long-term reaction of citizens to their experience with education is also impacted by external stimuli, such as economic crises, which have the capacity to radically transform the public's view of their past lived experiences, especially given the power of mass media to obscure the nature and cause of the crisis.

The focus of this section is in showing how the mass media has guided the political discourse part of the cycle by attributing the economic crisis to defects in the education system, through its episodic portrayals of inept teachers needing to be saved by a virtuous outsider (Ayers, 2001; Edling, 2014; Goldstein, 2011). The preponderance of this good/bad teacher duality has been a recurring theme in both popular culture media and news media coverage, serving to both prefigure and reify the view of teachers laid out in *A Nation at Risk*. This view effectively flattens the teacher experience, as it treats the profession in a non-relational way (Edling, 2014).

This binary is also glimpsed in a recurrent popular culture trope pointing an accusatory finger at teachers. Ayers (2001) charts the existence of this trope through Hollywood movies from the 1950s through to the 1990s, which tend to portray teachers as incompetent, with the exception of the outsider who swoops in to save the children. He starts with the 1955 film *Blackboard Jungle*, which depicts civilization doing battle with savagery in the form of a white liberal reformer joining the ranks of teachers in a dysfunctional and violent inner-city school, ultimately saving the desperate damsel of a female teacher in addition to the disorderly teenagers. In the 1974 film *Conrack*, the white savior moves to an island off the coast of South Carolina to whip the locals into shape, who are fortunate that the hero is immune from the deficiencies that seem to plague everyone else (Ayers, 2001). Meanwhile, the 1989 film *Lean on Me* depicts Morgan Freeman as a hero that Ayers describes as having an irrational devotion to the work of bringing order and discipline to the lawless high school (Ayers, 2001).

More recently, the outside savior trope recurred in the weekly television series, *Boston Public*. In this case, an ineffective black principal and administration is posed in contradistinction to teachers who enter the scene as "great white hopes who know what is best for all students, but particularly African American and low-income students" (Tillman & Trier, 2007, pp. 127–128). Tillman and Trier note that the impression that is left by this phenomenon is that teaching is a profession that anyone can do, despite abundant evidence suggesting that teachers with proper training fare markedly better than those who come in without a background in education. For example, Darling-Hammond and Sykes (2003) note that teachers with no student teaching experience vacate their jobs at "rates twice as high as those who have had such practice teaching" (p. 5).

Nonetheless, the outside savior has been realized in practice via Teach for America (TFA): a non-profit that places recent college graduates into teaching positions in underserved communities under a public service guise. Lahann and Reagan (2011) characterize TFA as embodying "progressive neoliberalism": that is, a logic "embracing neoliberalism's focus on deregulation, business strategies, and the managerial culture of accountability, but working to fight inequality and to reform the systems which produced it" (p. 20). In other words, TFA embodies the contradictions undergirding neoliberal education: pretending to fight inequities while embracing the logics that gave rise to them in the first place. Because market logics have been so successfully naturalized, participants in this program do not readily see this contradiction in plain view.

When not portraying teachers and administrators as broadly inept and ineffective, they are variously depicted as lazy, cynical, and reactionary: all characteristics seen in the two main teachers of the *The Simpsons*, as described by Kantor et al. (2001). Lisa Simpson's teacher, Elizabeth Hoover, is depicted as a dinosaur stubbornly impervious to change. Edna Krabappel, meanwhile, has shown a bit more complexity of character, though her principal purpose, at the end of the day, is as nemesis and roadblock to Bart. Moreover, the show repeatedly plays on the theme of school as a limiting institution: one that serves only to file students into a narrow range of potential future professions.

Opportunities to break free of the restraints of these permanent fixtures are limited, though one episode depicts an outside savior in the form of Mr. Bergstrom: a substitute teacher that Lisa fawns over because of his unconventional approach and intellectual passions. He is everything that her world is not: a contrast brought into sharp relief when Homer embarrasses Lisa in front of him during a chance encounter at a museum (Kantor et al., 2001).

In this formulation, the known world is one of limited possibility and restraint. Breaking free requires an outside intervention, because the dysfunctional schools and uninspired staff in place are simply not up to the task of elevating students to the level of achievement necessary to compete in today's global economy (Berliner & Biddle, 1995; Cohen, 2010). The effect of this narrative on educational discourse is to treat schools primarily as an instrument of class ascendance: that is, of a mechanism to free people from the economic conditions they were born into. As such, educational performance is discursively tied to economic performance in the dominant narratives and tropes of popular culture coverage.

It figures, then, that the crisis theme would be amplified as economic opportunities began to narrow in the 1970s, with the United States exiting a thirty-year long period of economic expansion. This was precisely the finding of Berliner and Biddle (1995), who chart the discursive attack by the political and media elite on schools and teachers beginning in this era. In the face of falling tax revenues, political leaders increasingly looked to balance budgets by enacting cuts in education, which were justified through the implementation of the crisis narrative (Berliner & Biddle, 1995).

This process accelerated after publication of *A Nation at Risk*, which they argue was reported largely uncritically in the press: "This document was reported in literally hundreds of newspaper and television accounts across the nation, and as far as we can tell, none of those reports noted its lack of citations or called for documentation of its incendiary charges. As a result, the public was led to believe that the claims it made were unimpeachable" (p. 169). The report had aligned so neatly with the existing narrative about school dysfunction and teacher incompetence that the findings were taken at face value, thus re-contextualizing the existing popular culture trope into a news media frame.

The function of this frame has been two-fold: on the one hand, to naturalize the crisis narrative, and, on the other hand, to hold individual schools and teachers accountable for the crisis (Anderson, 2007; Berliner & Biddle, 1995; Cohen, 2010; Goldstein, 2014). In employing Iyengar's (1991) typology, coverage of education has tended to be "episodic" rather than "thematic" in nature, where the former focuses on individual iterations of a problem as exemplars of the bigger issue, and the latter frames the problem as being systemic in nature. By generally focusing on anecdotes of inept traditional teachers, and outside saviors as veritable panaceas, the issue of underachievement in education was stripped of its structural roots (Anderson, 2007; Rooks & Bank-Munoz, 2015). In this frame, teacher and student performance is conflated with test scores, rather than seeing the latter as a function of economic conditions prevailing in the surrounding districts, or of sociological biases working against the student population. Anderson (2007) notes that this approach comports with a more general conservative tendency to value order as the principal resolutions to problems. In describing this conservative value-set and how it bears on education policy, Lakoff (2004) says:

Because immoral, undisciplined children can lead moral, disciplined children astray, parents should be able to choose to which school they send their children. Government funding should be taken from public schools and given to parents in the form of vouchers. This will help wealthier (more disciplined and moral) citizens send their children to private or religious schools that teach conservative values and impose appropriate discipline. (pp. 83–84)

In other words, the teacher accountability frame is itself rooted in a "strict father" frame that serves as legitimation for existing class stratification. By this view, wealth is a reflection of innate personality traits, first and foremost. Predictably, then, poverty tends to be treated in a similarly episodic nature according to Iyengar's (1991) study, with the poor being viewed as responsible for their own fate more than other societal subgroups (including the unemployed).

This correspondence between framing of poverty and education is no coincidence, moreover, given education's contradictory relation to economic achievement. As mentioned earlier, one of the core assumptions about education emerging from the pedagogical literature is the conflicting role it plays in legitimating existing economic hierarchies while also privileging an openness to a diversity of knowledge and perspectives that hold the potential to undermine these hierarchies by offering opportunities to all (Bernstein, 1990; Bowles & Gintis, 1976). Bowles and Gintis (1976) describe these as the "integrative" and "egalitarian" functions of education, respectively, noting that the former tends to drape itself in a meritocratic façade so that it seems to act like the latter. The result is that education is expected to accomplish that which it cannot possibly do, i.e. permit all that apply themselves the opportunity to climb the class ladder.

This tension between the integrative and egalitarian functions explains the tendency to fault the education system for social problems that are largely external to it. By viewing education as the principal mechanism of meritocratic advancement, I argue that the public is primed to see educational dysfunction as the cause of economic crises. People assume that because personal success is a meritocratic function of educational performance, then the obverse condition must be true for society as a whole: the nation's economic struggles must be indicative of failings throughout the whole of the education system. Moreover, given that poverty tends to be attributed to individual deficiencies (Iyengar, 1991), so too are problems with education.

This tendency to fault the individual for broader social problems is reflective of a subjective shift from classical liberalism to neoliberalism (Apple, 2001; Olssen, 1996). Olssen (1996) notes that classical liberalism tends to herald a self-interested economic actor as the core subject, whereas neoliberalism favors an active role for the state in forging a "manipulatable man." He explains:

> In an age of universal welfare, the perceived possibilities of slothful indolence create necessities for new forms of vigilance, surveillance, 'performance appraisal' and other forms of control generally. In this model the state has taken it upon itself to keep us all up to the mark (p. 340).

None of this is to suggest that the educational realm does not have its problems. Nor is it to deny that a crisis, of sorts, exists. Instead, I argue that the nature and cause of the crisis boils down to ideological questions. Neoconservatives will tend to fault a lack of order and discipline in school systems for society's problems, whereas neoliberals will point to a curriculum that is not adequately geared toward corporate needs, while progressives and leftists will tend to frame educational deficiencies as reflective of larger social injustices, such as the inequality of funding between schools in poor and affluent districts (Anderson, 2007).

The dominant ideologies seen in the media frames unpacked in this section reside in both neoconservative and neoliberal ideologies. The former is reflected in Hollywood tropes depicting unruly children, where vice has taken hold of young people, and regular teachers are powerless to subdue them without an outside savior. Meanwhile, the neoliberal frame is seen in the view that the stagnant American economy was caused by a burdensomely bloated public sphere. In the interdiscursive model of education policy and practice developed in this article, the media-dominant realm of political discourse is colored by a marriage of convenience between these two political strands. Together, they represent the ideologies of the dominant social order that emerged out of the structural crises of the 1970s (Apple, 2001; Hardt & Negri, 2000). The next section will delineate the nature of those crises, and how they came to determine the discourses around education, their framing in the media, and the resulting policy and practice.

On the Relationship Between Structure and Practice

An appreciation of social structure is vital to understanding the dynamics of educational practice, owing to the first assumption about the function of education in society laid out earlier. Specifically, political discourse and education practice are intrinsically interrelated, as the latter is reflected in the former over struggles over policy and structure in education. It is through this struggle that discourses are ultimately re-contextualized and transferred from the political to the educational realm. This contested process reveals most vividly education's contradictory functions of legitimation and critical inquiry. Apple (2006) relates:

> Education is a site of struggle and compromise. It serves as a proxy as well for larger battles over what our institutions should do, whom they should serve, and who should make these decisions. And yet, by itself it is one of the major arenas in which resources, power, and ideology specific to policy, finance, curriculum, pedagogy and evaluation in education are worked through. Thus, education is both cause and effect, determining and determined. (p. 30)

American education saw a crisis emerge precisely because the society that encompassed it was faced with a crisis of its own. As already mentioned, Berliner and Biddle (1995) located the outgrowth of the educational crisis talk as occurring during the end of the era of great economic expansion in the 1970s, when pressures began to mount to cut public expenditures in education, while, concomitantly, an evaluative culture emerged as a means of justifying these cuts (Apple, 2001), as discussed in the previous chapter.

However, I am not suggesting that the structural crisis determined the ensuing neoliberal turn in education policy, but, rather, that the context of crisis conditioned the discourses that emerged. My argument is that the "crisis of education" narrative arose out of the economic malaise of the day, as discourses began to center on uncovering a scapegoat for the nation's declining industrial competitiveness. In this quest, one dominant tendency of both the political and media elite was to frame poor education standards as the primary culprit (Berliner & Biddle, 1995). In sum, the crisis narrative served to naturalize the ensuing neoliberal reforms, whose principal effect has been the fortification of the elite in the world's leading economies (Harvey, 2005; Piketty, 2014). The success of this project is seen in the rising income and wealth inequality in most industrialized countries over the past forty years, and also glimpsed in the rise of oligarchies in China, Russia, and many developing countries in which neoliberal policies have been prescribed (Harvey, 2005). As an example, Piketty (2014) notes that, between 1977 and 2007, 75% of growth in the U.S. economy went to the top 10%, with a full 60% being captured by the top 1%. Harvey (2005) relates:

> Neoliberalism has not been very effective in revitalizing global capital accumulation, but it has succeeded remarkably well in restoring, or in some instances (as in Russia and China) creating, the power of an economic elite. The theoretical utopianism of neoliberal argument has, I conclude, primarily worked as a system of justification and legitimation for whatever needed to be done to achieve this goal. (p. 19).

Likewise, the discourses promulgated by elites around education reform served the same legitimating function. However, it is important to note that society did not neatly bifurcate between elite and marginalized groups during this process. In fact, many members of the latter have embraced these reforms for offering opportunities to escape underfunded and dysfunctional public school systems, even if the alternatives effectively re-inscribe market logics that largely work to disadvantage these groups (Apple, 1996; Lipman, 2011). In the same manner, testing has often been viewed as a means of class ascension by poor and minority populations lacking any other viable path to economic betterment (Hartman, 2003).

In this respect, I endorse Stuart Hall's (1985) notion of there being "no necessary correspondence" between a class of people and any specific ideology, so that "determinacy is transferred from the genetic origins of class or other social forces in a structure to the effects or results of a practice" (p. 95). In this formulation, structure is viewed as "previously structured practices" that serve to develop the conditions existent at the beginning of a narrative (p. 95). In this case, the story begins with a crisis of capitalism that precipitated a discursive and ideological turn to neoliberal logics seeking to rein in public expenditures and introduce market discipline into the public sector as a means for the economic elite to recapture lost standing. Meanwhile, the reforms were enacted in such a way as to often address real problems with the old model, such as in providing alternative charter schools in communities wherein the local public schools had suffered years of underfunding and neglect (Lipman, 2011).

From the "Crisis of Education" to the "Battle for the Soul of Education"

This fundamental crisis of American hegemony and industrial capitalism injected itself into the interdiscursive flow of signs and symbols that serves as the framework guiding this research, embedding a sense of limitation into the psyche of the nation, thus precipitating discourses of despair, evinced most lucidly in the political realm via the publication of *A Nation at Risk* (Goldstein, 2014). While many critical commentators certainly recognized the structural roots of the crisis, the mass media tended to draw on pre-existing tropes of the savagery lurking in the nation's schools as the source of the malaise. From Hollywood films to major television series, teachers were variously portrayed as inept, boring, old-fashioned, and restraining (Ayers, 2001; Berliner & Biddle, 1995; Goldstein, 2014; Kantor et al, 2001; Tillman & Trier, 2007). These portrayals served to reinforce the discourses of crisis wherein economic problems were tied directly to teacher and student performance.

It is here that the gulf between the thematic and episodic news framing of education becomes particularly significant. By privileging the latter in its coverage, the commercial news media reduced a complex structural crisis to a trivial technical problem that could be solved with a healthy dose of market discipline. Anywhere and everywhere, the public was perceived as inefficient, wasteful, and inept. It needed to be brought into line.

While this frame of a wayward public sector worked to convince large parts of the population of the need for neoliberal reforms, it also ultimately stoked resentment among those impacted by the decades-long assault on public education. The willingness of so many teachers in recent years to contest the market rationalizations of education represents a significant break with the dominant discourses and tropes surrounding the form and function of schooling in this country. Their capacity to also mobilize mass movements around the issues further points to an exhausting of the neoliberal hegemonic consensus.

Indeed, CORE's success is informed by its emphasis on sharing and discussing ideas about the relationship of schools to the communities they are embedded in. Specifically, its early efforts of organizing reading groups in which the larger issue of neoliberalism and its effects on the urban environment were discussed helped build lasting bridges with community groups that proved organizationally fruitful (Ashby & Bruno, 2016; Brogan, 2014). This practice continued in 2012 as the strike neared, during which they organized teach-ins to educate people on the reasons for the strike, while countering unsympathetic mainstream media framing of their organizing efforts (Brogan, 2014).

This privileging of information is part of a more extensive embrace of greater democratization by CORE. This focus has translated into expanding the bargaining committee to 60 people, while also opening it up to greater transparency (Brogan, 2014). Meanwhile, in viewing their concerns as being interlinked with those of their communities, they have built coalitions with a range of neighborhood groups, most notably through the Grassroots Education Movement (GEM), as a vehicle through which to resist slated school closures (Ashby & Bruno, 2016; Brogan, 2014; Uetricht, 2014).

As elaborated further in Chapter 2, CORE pushed the CTU in more of a "social movement unionism" direction. Rather than focusing narrowly on contractual demands, their struggle, in the words of CTU president Karen Lewis, has been about the very "soul of education" (Ashby & Bruno, 2016; Uetricht, 2014).

It is also worth noting that the emphasis on school-community relations was an advisable tack to take in the critique of neoliberal reforms, given the fact that there is no broad consensus among teachers and parents on what exactly needs to be done as far as structuring schools and their systems of testing and evaluation. As mentioned earlier, many members of marginalized communities have embraced these reforms, for the very fact that they represent change from an undesirable status quo (Lipman, 2011). Charter schools, in particular, are viewed as more accessible versions of the exclusive "magnet schools," which base entry on test results and have been built to cater to elite populations in the city. In this way, magnets have effectively "primed the pump" for the ensuing "charterization" (Lipman, 2011). Furthermore, the occasional charter has been organized by progressive groups embracing a pedagogy privileging critical thinking and cultural awareness, such as the Betty Shabazz charter school in Chicago (Lipman, 2011).

As such, CORE's principal message has not been one of opposition to charter schools, per se, but rather on their use to undermine traditional public schools and the teaching corps employed there. They view neoliberal reforms as motivated by a desire to bring education policy in line with the dictates of powerful interests that see education as a threat. The battle for the "soul of education" is one rooted in a belief among teachers that education should not serve the interests of the powerful but should instead be a conduit through which all citizens are capable of realizing their full potential, while also gaining the skills necessary to be members of an engaged citizenry (Ashby & Bruno, 2016).

In this section, I have delineated the history of this cycle of communication from crisis to contestation. The story began with the economic crisis of the 1970s, which precipitated the neoliberal turn to lean government as part of a process of elite entrenchment. In order to justify public spending cuts, policymakers sought a scapegoat, for which they drew on pre-existing tropes about the ineptitude of teachers and the barbarity of public school populations. In addition to cuts, reforms have mandated continual evaluation of student progress as a marker of the performance of both schools and teachers, which has served as a rationalization for the closures of traditional public schools, largely in underserved urban communities, the opening of privately run charters to replace them, and the concomitant turn to a mostly non-unionized teaching staff in these alternative schools. In response, teachers in a number of locations have mounted campaigns to push back on these reforms: efforts that have married community concerns about the fate of local public schools to teacher concerns about the broader function of schools in society.

A Discursive Struggle

I contend that this wave of teacher uprisings marks the latest realization of education as a site of struggle. However, the struggle is not merely a political one over working conditions and contract demands, but also a discursive one over how we make sense of the world around us, owing to the fact that education constitutes one of the central institutions involved in the production and reproduction of ideological hegemony (Apple, 1995). This is to say that prevailing value systems in any society are partially reflected and partially formed in this struggle over the soul of education. Market logics have been reflected in the educational realm via a process of successive re-contextualizations from media trope to political rhetoric to public policy. In response, a counter-frame has emerged in the actions of teachers, permitting a synthesis of the dominant view with one that sees education as a bedrock of the community: a place that should serve the neighborhood it is embedded in, rather than a market that is external to it.

It is also important to note that this counter-frame has emerged in a time of opening of discursive space across the world, in which once moribund political ideologies have returned to the fore (on both the left and right side of the spectrum), and a palpable sense of frustration has risen in countries throughout the world. From Brexit to the election of Trump and other nationalists of the same flavor throughout the world to the resurgence of a long-moribund democratic socialism in places like the United States and United Kingdom, populations have repeatedly expressed their disaffection with the neoliberal center and its politics of transferring sovereignty to outside forces: be it global finance or Brussels or Washington, D.C.

In other words, the current teachers' struggle is part of a broader crisis of neoliberalism: a hegemonic break in which cultural institutions, like schools, are realizing heightened importance in the reformulation of dominant logics. This is because, as Apple (2013) notes:

> Educational institutions are not apart from society. They are central elements of that society—as work places, as sites of identity formation, as places that make particular knowledge and culture legitimate, as arenas of mobilization and learning of tactics, and so much more. (p. 159)

Nonetheless, he notes that the process of transforming society through education requires sustained collective action, which also necessitates a recognition of how conservative forces have used education policy as a mechanism of change themselves (Apple, 2013). In other words, educators must appreciate the fact that they operate in a domain of ongoing discursive struggle over ideological hegemony in society. In this sense, the battle for the soul of education is also a battle over how we interpret the world around us, what type of knowledge gets privileged, what social problems receive attention, and how society is constituted in addressing those problems.

References

Althusser, L. (1971/2014). *On the reproduction of capitalism: Ideology and ideological state apparatuses.* Verso.

Anderson, G. (2007). Media's impact on educational policies and practices: Political spectacle and social control. *Peabody Journal of Education*, *82*(1), 103–120.
Apple, M. (1995). *Education and power* (2nd ed.). Routledge.
Apple, M. (1996). *Cultural politics and education*. Teachers College Press.
Apple, M. (2001). *Educating the right way: Markets, standards, god, and inequality*. Routledge.
Apple, M. (2006). *Educating the right way*. Routledge.
Apple, M. (2013). *Can education change society?* Routledge.
Ashby, S., & Bruno, R. (2016). *A fight for the soul of public education: The story of the Chicago teachers strike*. Cornell University Press.
Ayers, W. (2001). A Teacher ain't nothin' but a hero: Teachers and teaching in film. In P. B. Joseph & G. Burnaford (Eds.), *Images of Schoolteachers in America* (pp. 201–210). Lawrence Erlbaum Associates.
Bennett, W. L., & Graber, D. A. (2007). *News: The politics of illusion*. Pearson Longman.
Berliner, D., & Biddle, B. (1995). *The manufactured crisis: Myths, fraud and the attack on America's public schools*. Addison-Wesley.
Bernstein, B. (1990). *The Structuring of Pedagogic Discourse*. Routledge.
Bowles, S., & Gintis, H. (1976). *Schooling in capitalist America: Educational reform and the contradictions of economic life*. Basic Books.
Brogan, P. (2013). Education in global Chicago and the remaking of contemporary capitalism. *The Canadian Geographer/le Geographe Canadien*, *57*(3), 303–310.
Brogan, P. (2014). Getting to the CORE of the Chicago Teachers' Union transformation. *Studies in Social Justice*, *8*(2), 145–164.
Cohen, J. (2010). Teachers in the news: A critical analysis of one US newspaper's discourse on education, 2006–2007. *Discourse: Studies in the Cultural Politics of Education*, *31*(1), 105–119.
Darling-Hammond, L., & Skyes G. (2003). Wanted: A national teacher supply policy for education: The right way to meet the "highly qualified teacher" challenge. Education Policy Analysis Archives, 11(33).
Delli Carpini, M. X., & Williams, B. A. (2001). Let us infotain you: Politics in the new media age. In W. L. Benne & R. M. Entman (Eds.), *Mediated politics: Communication in the future of democracy* (pp. 160–181). Cambridge University Press.
Edling, S. (2014). Between curriculum complexity and stereotypes: Exploring stereotypes of teachers and education in media as a question of structural violence. *J. Curriculum Studies*, *47*(3), 399–415.
Gitlin, T. (2003). *The whole world is watching: Mass media in the making and unmaking of the new left*. The University of California Press.

Goldstein, D. (2014). *The teacher wars: A history of America's most embattled profession.* Doubleday.
Goldstein, R. (2011). Imaging the frame: Media representations of teachers, their unions, NCLB, and education reform. *Educational Policy, 25*(4), 543–576.
Gramsci, A. (1971). In Q. Hoare, & G. Nowell-Smith (Eds.), *Selections from the prison notebooks of Antonio Gramsci.* International Publishers.
Hall, S. (1985). Signification, representation, ideology: Althusser and the post-structuralist debates. *Critical Studies in Media Communication, 2*(2), 91–114.
Hall, S. (2013). *Policing the crisis: Mugging, the state, and law and order* (2nd ed.). Palgrave Macmillan.
Hall, S. (2016). Cultural studies 1983: A theoretical history. Durham, NC: Duke University Press.
Hardt, M., & Negri, A. (2000). *Empire.* Harvard University Press.
Hartman, A. (2003). The social production of American identity: Standardized testing reform in the United States. *Socialism and Democracy, 17*(2), 131–164.
Harvey, D. (2005). *A Brief history of neoliberalism.* Oxford University Press.
Herman, E. S., & Chomsky, N. (1988). *Manufacturing consent: The political economy of the mass media.* Pantheon Books.
Iyengar, S. (1991). *Is Anyone Responsible?: How television frames political issues.* University of Chicago Press.
Kantor, K., Kantor, N. L., Kantor, J., Eaton, M., & Kantor, B. (2001). "I will not expose the ignorance of the faculty": The Simpsons as school satire. In P. B. Joseph & G. Burnaford (Eds.), *Images of Schoolteachers in America* (2nd ed., pp. 185–200). Lawrence Erlbaum Associates.
Kellner, D., & Share, J. (2007). Critical media literacy, democracy, and the reconstruction of education. In D. Macedo & S. R. Steinberg (Eds.), *Media literacy: A reader* (pp. 3–23). Peter Lang Publishing.
Lahann, R., & Reagan, E. M. (2011). Teach for America and the politics of progressive neoliberalism. *Teacher Education Quarterly, 38*(1), 7–27.
Lakoff, G. (2004). *Don't think of an elephant! Know your values and frame the debate: The essential guide for progressives.* Chelsea Green Pub. Co.
Lipman, P. (2011). *The new political economy of urban education: Neoliberalism, race, and the right to the city.* Routledge.
Olssen, M. (1996). In defense of the welfare state and of publicly provided education. *Journal of Education, 11*(3), 337–362.
Piketty, T. (2014). *Capital in the twenty-first century.* Harvard University Press.
Rooks, D., & Munoz, C. B. (2015). Brilliant, bored or badly behaved? Media coverage of the charter school debate in the United States. *Teachers College Record, 117,* Article 080302.
Thomas, S. (2011). Teachers and public engagement: An argument for rethinking teacher professionalism to challenge deficit discourses in the

public sphere. *Discourse: Studies in the Cultural Politics of Education, 32*(3), 371–382.

Tillman, L., & Trier, J. (2007). Boston Public as public pedagogy: Implications for teacher preparation and school leadership. *Peabody Journal of Education, 82*(1), 121–149.

Uetricht, M. (2014). *Strike for America*. Verso.

Walgrave, S., & Van Aelst, P. (2006). The contingency of the mass media's political agenda setting power: Toward a preliminary theory. *Journal of Communication, 56*(1), 88–109.

CHAPTER 6

Teachers in the Networks of Crowd Mobilization

Abstract This chapter examines the various ways that participants in the 2018 uprising used Facebook to organize and promote the movement, focusing on the organizational capacities of social media in harnessing movement growth. The methodology employed involved culling Facebook posts from a selected date range around the various uprisings and then categorizing the resulting images. I inductively established four categories of purpose that reflect the technological affordances of the platform. It further argues that activists should think tactically about how their various movements could apply these affordances to their respective movements, rather than glorifying digital communication technologies and their capacity to build movements. It would be far more beneficial to have a balanced view that recognizes the existence of very specific uses that can be made of social media platforms, while recognizing the dangers of a technologically deterministic viewpoint that negates the importance of building larger real-world structures.

Keywords Facebook use by social movements · Facebook use by teacher unions · Facebook use by teacher activists · Social media and activism

© The Author(s), under exclusive license to Springer Nature Switzerland AG 2025
M. Reichel, *Teacher Power in the Digital Age*, Social Movements and Transformation, https://doi.org/10.1007/978-3-031-87191-7_6

In the last chapter, I argued that messaging and meaning are integral components of the teachers' movement: that this is a movement, in large part, about how society should think about education and the various issues educators are currently confronting. By extension, the way teacher activists have communicated amongst each other, and with the general public, is an important part of this story. As argued in Chapter 2, the communicative and organizational interventions of this movement have been vital in realizing significant success in this struggle, while also marking the beginnings of a sectoral shift toward "social movement unionism" on the part of participating union members.

I mentioned, then, that much of this communication strategy has occurred on the digital pathways of social media, though I did not get into the details of how exactly social media was used by activists. This chapter will delve into the details through an empirical investigation of the major state-wide Facebook groups used during the 2018 uprising. The findings of this investigation indicate that social media can serve a purpose throughout the entire cycle of contention of a movement: from articulating the cause to mobilizing the ranks, to motivating movement participants to continue their involvement to discussion and evaluation of the status of the movement. I contend that these are vital components to the communicative intervention teacher activists have made in pushing their unions in a more contentious direction, while also being more responsiveness to union structures that had become more quite insulated from its rank-and-file with the business unionism that has prevailed throughout the neoliberal era.

Identifying Purpose in Social Media Practice

I focused this investigation on three of the four most prominent statewide movements of 2018: those in West Virginia, Oklahoma, Arizona. The fourth state, Kentucky, was ultimately left out of the study due to the fact that Facebook usage there was scattered across dozens of county-level Facebook pages, whereas the other states all had active state-level pages for much of the duration of the movement activity.

For each of the three states, I surveyed posts among the groups dedicated to organizing, rather than the ones set up for other explicit purposes, such as discussion (though discussion-oriented posts were seen rather commonly in states that did not designate a group specifically for that purpose). In each case, I selected posts between the creation of the group online and the end of high-traffic activity on the group page, or the end of June 2018, whichever came sooner. I deemed a post "high-traffic" if it received at least twenty forms of engagement of any sort, i.e. likes, shares or comments. In the case of the WV United Caucus, the resulting date range was February 26, 2018 to May 16, 2018. Before then, there were other Facebook groups involved in organizing, but that was the first date wherein the movement was consolidated into one group. For the Oklahoma Teachers United, the selected date range was February 10, 2018 to May 10, 2018. Lastly, I used March 7th, 2018 until June 30th, 2018 for Arizona Educators United. High traffic activity continued after that end date due to the fact that teachers pivoted from their walkout campaign to an "Invest in Ed" ballot initiative that would have required high income earners to pay higher income taxes to cover proposed increases in education spending. This initiative was ultimately deemed unconstitutional in 2021 for exceeding constitutional spending limits (Duda & Small, 2021).

I extracted qualifying posts from the selected date ranges by taking a screenshot, and then proceeded to survey and categorize the resulting images. I inductively established categories during the survey process in a three-part process. Firstly, I provided broad descriptors of what each individual post was doing, and, as I noted certain tendencies, I combined individual posts into groups based on common themes, such as "expressions of solidarity from outside the movement," a category that involved both images and messages of support from any non-teacher, including other union workers, celebrities or political figures. I then combined these thematic categories into larger groupings based on the purpose of posts, ultimately coming up with four categories of purpose: "narration of cause," "mobilization," "motivation," and "discussion/information sharing."

The "narration of cause" posts were those that I felt most closely created the emotional resonance that Gerbaudo (2012) discusses. This content articulated (or re- articulated) the central cause(s) of the movement by discussing some of the underlying issues in emotive and/ or personal ways. They included posts that: shared and reacted to news updating on the struggle; communicated a personal background story and why it highlights the need for the movement; and sounded off on a particular issue.

The next category of purpose—"mobilization"—was the most straightforward to identify. These posts shared details about a specific event or course of action: an invitation to join a Facebook event page or a plea to take action in some other way, such as by signing an online petition for a cause related to the movement.

I decided to call the third category "motivation," as it involves posts rallying followers to sustain and grow the movement. In the end, this category was the most numerically prominent of the four, suggesting that this function may have been most useful for activists organizing on Facebook. However, I would refrain from making too far-reaching a conclusion based on this fact, as the preponderance of "motivation" posts might be mostly attributable to the timing of when the state-wide Facebook groups that I surveyed were created: i.e., after the initial phase of recruitment and mobilization had passed on local and county level groups. These posts include messages of solidarity and support from other teachers involved in the movement, both within the state and in other states active in the movement, as well as from people outside of the movement. The content included pictures and videos of teachers from various rallies or walkouts within the given state; pictures of signs from the rallies; and text statements communicating support.

The final category I identified was "discussion/ information sharing," which encompasses posts with a neutral, information-sharing tone. These posts were not designed to convince followers to think a certain way about the issue, per se, as much as they were intended to simply provide details about a certain issue, or to seek responses on a query of some sort (polls were included in this category).

I then tabulated results from each of the categories in each state and provided a qualitative analysis of the data. The tabulation gives an idea of the prevalence of each category of purpose among posts in each state, while highlighting some of the differences in how activists used Facebook across those states. Meanwhile, the qualitative analysis allows for these data to come to life: that is, for each of the fundamental purposes of these posts to be highlighted with specific examples that serve to tell the story of the movement through the ways in which Facebook was used by its participants.

A Heuristic of Social Media Purpose

While the existing literature on social media use by social movements emphasizes the affective register of social media use by movements, I argue that emotional appeals were mostly useful in the initial recruitment of teachers to the movement and occasionally in subsequent posts geared toward motivating the masses. The other two sides of the movement cycle (illustrated in the figure below), involved posts that tended to be dispassionate and informative in tone.

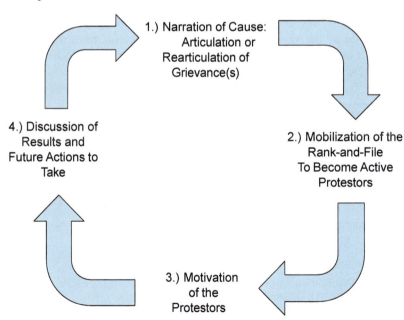

It is important to note that this typology is simply a heuristic to help in understanding a highly complex communicative environment: posts did not strictly follow this sequence, though there was a tendency in this direction. Moreover, I believe the order makes sense as something of an organic progression for the life cycle of a movement: Firstly, recruit adherents to the movement through an emotive narration of the underlying cause; secondly, mobilize followers to become active participants; thirdly, motivate them to stay involved as protests continue and pressure mounts on the union infrastructure and the governing officials they are in negotiation with; lastly, engage in discussion about where the movement stands before potentially restarting the cycle of contestation.

That said, posts of all types could be found at any point in the timeline of the movement. "Discussion/ information" posts, in particular, tended to occur throughout the life cycle, owing to the fact that this category included miscellaneous posts, rather than just the reflective posts highlighted in the schematic above. Some miscellaneous examples include a protestor looking for an item lost at a rally, messages from journalists seeking interview subjects from the movement, and questions posed by individual members to the group about specific protest tactics or messages to put on signs.

Nonetheless, my contention is that discussion posts took on added prominence at the end of the protest cycle, wherein there was a need for reflection and analysis before pushing forward with the next round of actions (Fig. 6.1).

CoP:	WEST VIRGINIA	OKLAHOMA	ARIZONA
NARRATION OF CAUSE	19	31	7
MOTIVATION	64	20	25
MOBILIZATION	3	14	29
DISCUSSION/ INFORMATION	21	17	30

Fig. 6.1 Distribution of posts by category of purpose in state level Facebook groups during 2018 uprising

The variation in the types of post employed in each state is less a function of any fundamental differences in the usage of the platform in the state as a whole, and more a result of the fact that the principal statewide Facebook group that I inspected came into existence at different stages in the progression of the movement in those states. For example, the lack of "narration of cause" posts in Arizona is a result of the fact that most of the original recruitment of followers occurred in the individual district pages, prior to the implementation of the statewide group page. Meanwhile, in West Virginia, there was a dearth of mobilization posts, owing to the fact that the statewide group was made public after the first wave of mobilizations had already occurred, and, thus, the focus shifted largely to motivation of participants in the date range that I captured in this study. As such, Oklahoma produced the most representative sample across all categories of purpose, due to the fact that I was able to grab a set of dates that covered the entire cycle of contestation, and none of the categories of purpose occurred on other group pages.

Together, the sampling of posts used in this study effectively tell a compelling story about the role of social media in this uprising, which I will now flesh out in a category-by- category analysis.

NARRATION OF CAUSE

The Oklahoma Teachers United set produces the most representative posts for this category, owing to the fact that the main Oklahoma group page, "Oklahoma Teachers United," was implemented in time to capture initial articulations of the movement's cause. The following post is an exemplar of this initial phase of narrating the cause.

By comparison, the following screenshot exemplifies a *re-articulation* of the cause, posted just a few weeks after the post above, as teachers continued to mobilize despite receiving a pay raise.

This second example illustrates the emotive nature of this category of Facebook post, as the group admin expresses frustration with the ongoing impasse, in which some gains were won, but there continues to be a perceived lack of appreciation of the severity of teachers' plight on the part of the news media. Likewise, the following post from West.

Virginia heightened the level of emotional resonance by relating the underlying issues to the user's personal story.

This example also illustrates the fact that it was not just teachers involved in the movement, as organizers also included other school workers and public employees in their advocacy, recognizing that they have fallen victim to the same neoliberal forces that teachers have been subjected to.

As a whole, this "category of purpose" tended to be more personal and emotive than the other categories. It is here that other scholars investigating social media use by social movements are correct in saying that emotional resonance is important in constituting the movement. However, I contend that once activists were recruited, the tone of Facebook posts began to shift.

Mobilization

Once activists had been recruited into the movement via appeals narrating the cause, the next logical step was to mobilize them into action. It is here that the movement began to pivot from social media into the squares: what Gerbaudo (2012) describes as the *"material precipitation from symbolic assemblages to bodily assemblages in public space"* (p.42). This shift necessarily centered on translating the emotional energy into a congregation in the real world. In that sense, these posts were more logistical in nature: an invitation to join a rally or other event, or to sign a petition or donate to the cause.

Here are examples of each of these forms of mobilization:

6 TEACHERS IN THE NETWORKS OF CROWD MOBILIZATION 107

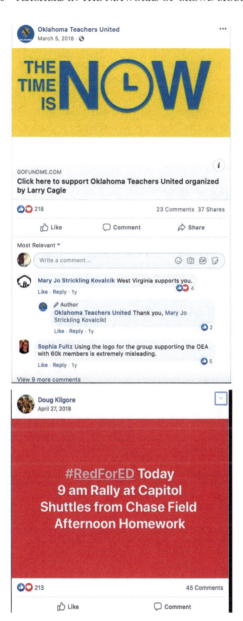

These examples all represent fairly straightforward efforts at mobilizing followers to specific purposes within the movement. However, the occasional message blurs the line between categories, insofar as it rearticulates the cause while also mobilizing for a specific purpose. In those cases, I had to make a judgment call based on that I determined the principal purpose of the post was. The missive below from Oklahoma Teachers United is one such example, as the organizer reiterates some of the core tenets of the movements' message before continuing on with detailed steps on how to respond to a specific set of circumstances.

Oklahoma Teachers United
March 31, 2018

EMERGENCY MESSAGE........COPY AND PASTE
SHARE AGAIN AND AGAIN
START PLANNING NOW!!!!!!!!!!!!!!!!!!!!!!! NOT ON MONDAY!!!!
OKLAHOMA STATEWIDE TEACHER WALKOUT
There is no going back, there is no backing down, no sitting down, no accepting last minute deals!!!!!!
WE ARE WALKING ON MONDAY!!!!!!THIS FIGHT FOR OUR SCHOOLS HAS BEGUN!!!!!!!!!!!!!!!!!!!!
This is a statewide referendum on the funding of our schools.

If Superintendents call districts back to work at any time after Monday we, the citizens of Oklahoma (Parents, students, teachers, community members) STAY UNITED.

#OKUNITED #SOLIDARITY

STEP 1:
If superintendents call teachers back to work, find groups of teachers in your school and call in sick and shut them down by FORCE!!! Organize with your teachers in groups of 5-15 and agree to call in at midnight for the following day. Repeat this with different groups so that not everyone uses up the same number of sick/personal days. WE DO THIS UNTIL THE END OF THE YEAR IF NECESSARY. Make those groups of teachers larger and larger until the school buckles.

STEP 2:
Get your parents to come to the school and go DIRECTLY INTO THE PRINCIPALS OFFICE and demand they shut the schools down!!!!!!! We want there to be so many parents in the lobby and in the principals office that there is NO WAY they can keep schools open.

STEP 3:
Get the names, emails, and phone numbers of your school board and superintendent and have media blitz parties in your homes and churches where parents, teachers, students, and members of our community send messages to these officials DEMANDING they close the schools.

While this last example operates at an emotional register, thus incorporating elements of "narration of cause" posts, it also contains explicit steps to be taken by followers, thus rendering it a part of the "mobilization" category of purpose. As a whole, this category tends toward the more dispassionate side, as the objective is relaying concrete steps followers could take.

Nonetheless, there was still room for emotional appeals as the movement pressed on and organizers sought to keep its adherents involved, as will be glimpsed in the next category.

Motivation

What separates "motivation" from "mobilization" in this typology is that the former starts to occur after some amount of mobilization has already taken place. At this point, the movement was underway, pressure was building on its political targets, and lead organizers sought to sustain the pressure by boosting the energy level of the movement's participants. The mechanisms of motivation took the form of expressions of solidarity and support from: teachers within the state, teachers in other states where the movement took hold, and people from outside the movement. In the former case, messages frequently contained images and videos from rallies or pickets that had already occurred, often with teachers holding signs. The message might also contain text rallying supporters to participate in an upcoming event, or relating a personal story designed to rally, rather than to re-articulate the cause (in which case the post would have been categorized as belonging to the "narration of cause" purpose). In the second case, a common message of motivation involved expressions of solidarity from or, on behalf of, the other states involved in the broader movement. These frequently involved images from protesters in those states, but also might take the form of a gesture making a nod to what is going on in the other states (such as a sign at a protest). In the case of outside support, messages of solidarity in all formats (text, image and video) come from other workers, parents, community members or celebrities.

Messages of motivation from within each state's movement were plentiful, usually involving colorful imagery from ongoing rally efforts, accentuating the sense of "collective effervescence" experienced in the squares. The following is an example of a video from Arizona wherein a sea of red-clad teachers take part in a rally at the Capitol Building in Phoenix:

Prior to that action, followers were encouraged to attend with the following motivating text message from one of the lead organizers, which is an example of another type of message of motivation from fellow in-state teacher activists:

Another variant of in-state "motivation" posts took the form of personal stories designed to rally the troops to action. The following is an example from West Virginia where a teacher undergoing treatment for cancer shares her message of solidarity. She also re-articulates the cause in her message—"We are real teachers who love our students and need affordable healthcare"—but this is a secondary purpose of the post, designed to augment the primary purpose of inspiring and motivating.

The second type of "motivation" post involved messages of solidarity between the various states involved in the uprising. In some cases, these posts reference all four of the major states involved in the 2018 uprising, sometimes with the hashtag #onepurpose, for those that were cross posted on other platforms. Others gave a nod to just one of the other states involved, with West Virginia being the most common of these, given its status as the pioneer of the movement:

The final type of Message of Motivation was far less common than the previous two, though they tended to get a lot of engagement, owing to the fact that they involve high-profile individuals, often celebrities from the entertainment world, expressing their solidarity with teachers.

These posts appeal to emotions in order to rally the ranks to further action by illustrating the broad-based support behind previous actions. In this respect, they demonstrate that the initial purpose has been achieved: that the articulation of the cause has resonated widely, resulting in a bona fide social movement.

However, the work was not complete at that stage, as pressure needed to be sustained so that the union infrastructure could succeed with its work. It is here that Facebook affords users the capacity to do that which was far more difficult in a prior era: easily communicate with one another in order to assess the progress that has been made so far.t

Discussion/Information

Despite the literature on social media-born social movements emphasizing emotion-generating images as the principal mechanism employed (Gerbaudo, 2012, 2017; Tufecki, 2017), the reality is that Facebook affords plenty of space for discussion and inquiry, owing to the fact that the platform makes it easy to pose questions and for members to then respond and continue the conversation in the comment section. The following example from the Arizona group vividly illustrates this functionality:

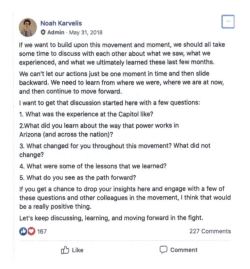

Within this category, posts would also occasionally focus on informing, rather than inquiring, though this certainly would not preclude the possibility of discussion in the comment section, which is always present. In this case, the Oklahoma Teachers United apprise its followers of the state of how successful its associated union was in achieving its stated demands:

Both of these posts make it clear that discussion posts are valuable as mechanisms to continue the discourse undergirding the movement into the next cycle, plainly vivified by Noah Karvelis above: "Let's keep discussing, learning, and moving forward in the fight."

These discussion posts may very well have been more important with the teachers' movement than the previous "movements of the squares," owing to the existence of an organization engaged in an actual legislative fight, so that there was more to assess and discuss in terms of concrete results. Indeed, discussion was the principal function through which the tension between the unions and the movement was addressed on social media. It was also through discussion that teachers could take stock of how far they succeeded in pushing their union infrastructure to change prevailing working conditions, while contemplating potential future courses of action. The movement would likely not have endured long enough to realize serious gains if not for Facebook's conversational affordances operating outside of an emotional register. These posts, like the union structure that teachers had, served to help anchor the movement, and prevent the sort of ephemerality that plagued other sectors of the "movements of the squares."

A Communicative Cycle of Contention

In this cycle of communicative purpose, an articulation of a cause was voiced, which then become the rallying cry of a social movement firmly situated within a larger historical wave of contention aimed at addressing the historic levels of inequality and precariousness of the neoliberal epoch. The teachers' movement effectively aired grievances related to pay, pensions, health care, education spending and a host of other issues, pushing further than their union leadership had in recent years. While not all demands were met, the movement was certainly more successful than earlier manifestations of the "movements of the squares." While those movements suffered from an ephemerality of a "crowd-enabled mobilization" lacking organizational structure, the teachers benefitted from having both "crowd-enabled" as well as "organizationally- enabled" features, to borrow from Bennett and Segerberg's (2013) typology mentioned in Chapter 2. The networking affordances of Facebook created a fresh communicative opening, permitting teachers to address a wider array of issues than those traditionally addressed in the collective bargaining process. While formal union channels—especially in recent years—severely limited the scope of issues that could be raised; in Facebook, teacher activists found tools with which they were able to connect around a broader range of grievances. Facebook's technological affordances permitted activists to articulate their cause, mobilize other disaffected teachers to action, motivate them to continue to keep up the pressure, and discuss the state of their movement. By engaging these tools, fueled by the resentment of neglect over the decades of neoliberal austerity, they succeeded in building one of the largest and most consequential strike waves in modern American history.

References

Bennett, L., & Segerberg, A. (2013). *The logic of connective action: Digital media and the personalization of contentious politics*. Cambridge, University Press.

Duda, J., & Small, J. (2021). Arizona Supreme Court sets the stage to overturn Prop 208 tax increase for school funding. *Arizona Mirror*. https://azmirror.com/2021/08/19/arizona-supreme-court-wont-block-prop-208-tax-increase-for-school-funding/

Gerbaudo, P. (2012). *Tweets and the streets: Social media and contemporary activism*. Pluto Press.

Gerbaudo, P. (2017). *The mask and the flag: Populism, citizenism and global protest*. Oxford University Press.

Tufecki, Z. (2017). *Twitter and tear gas: The power and fragility of networked protest*. Yale University Press.

CHAPTER 7

Teachers in the Dominant News Discourses

Abstract This chapter examines print news coverage of the teachers' movements from both the CTU strike of 2012 and the rolling uprising in 2018, focusing on discursive currents embedded in the dominant frames thereof. In so doing, it inspects how teachers and education are viewed in relation to problems existent in other sectors of society. In the end, the relatively sympathetic liberal frame became more prominent in the coverage of the 2018 strike wave, reflective of the success of teachers in using their "signifying power" to shift news media discourse on the role of education in society. Nonetheless, I argue that this shift did not effectively break with the neoliberal paradigm, because the coverage did not question why teachers were being blamed for problems outside of their control in the first place. Rarely was this context of the broader neoliberal offensive on organized labor ever provided as explanation for why these broader struggles in education were occurring in the first place.

Keywords News media framing of teacher strikes · News media framing of teachers · News media portrayals of education · Education and the media

While the last chapter looked at some of the practices undertaken by teacher activists as part of their broader communicative intervention,

© The Author(s), under exclusive license to Springer Nature Switzerland AG 2025
M. Reichel, *Teacher Power in the Digital Age*, Social Movements and Transformation, https://doi.org/10.1007/978-3-031-87191-7_7

this chapter turns the focus to the other side of the discursive flow from the heuristic presented in Chapter 5: the mass media discourses on educational issues. Given that the dominant media is largely owned and controlled by commercial interests, this tends to be a domain less favorable to social movement activity, though it is still responsive to popular pressure. This is to say that teachers are not in control of the messaging that occurs in this communicative orbit, though they can have an impact, as this empirical investigation ultimately suggests.

This study engages a frame analysis of dominant print news media coverage of both the 2012 Chicago teachers' strike and the 2018 rolling walkouts. In so doing, it builds upon previous work inspecting popular culture depictions of schools and teachers related in Chapter 5, wherein I discussed dominant tropes present in the depiction of teachers that frame education as a dysfunctional arena with inept teachers and administrators desperately in need of outside saviors to swoop in (Ayers, 2001; Kantor et al, 2001). In that chapter, I also argued that these tropes have paralleled the promulgation of the neoliberal reform which has essentially brought this narrative to life by disproportionately faulting teachers for social and economic problems largely outside of their control.

This chapter inspects a sampling of print news coverage from major national publications around both the 2012 Chicago teachers strike and the broader nation-wide walkout of 2018, looking for dominant themes, discursive currents, and tone that together serve to frame the larger narrative around the movement. Some of the guiding questions as I began this analysis included: To what extend does the coverage cast a disciplinary tone in its treatment of teachers? Are teachers disproportionately blamed for economic problems and other social issues in print coverage? What ideological tendencies are glimpsed in the coverage, and how do they reflect the breadth of elite reaction to the movement?

In fleshing out the dominant frames present in the coverage, I advance four core arguments. Firstly, the establishment news media frames generally reflect the overarching pro-corporate zeitgeist of the era, consistent with Herman and Chomsky's (1988) propaganda model that sees dominant news media as tending to overstate the elite ideology while obscuring or underreporting alternative viewpoints. Secondly, and relatedly, much of the coverage is devoid of any serious discussion of the issues that were motivating teachers, and when issues were raised, that discussion tended to trivialize matters, by, for example, focusing narrowly on teacher pay and not the myriad other issues that teachers were raising as part of these actions. This is consistent with how dominant news coverage of strikes has been historically in this country, as remarked by Walter Lippman (1922): "If you study the way many a strike is reported in the press, you will find, very often, that the issues are rarely in the headlines, barely in the leading paragraphs, and sometimes not even mentioned anywhere." Thirdly, there was a perceptible shift to more favorable coverage between 2012 and 2018, which I attribute to the institutional weight given to the nation-wide movement, as compared to the 2012 strike which was localized in one city, and which news media could dismiss as an isolated incident. Fourthly, I, nonetheless, contend that the more favorable coverage did not fundamentally challenge the dominant neoliberal paradigm in which educational discourses have been situated over the last 40–50 years. Instead, this coverage largely served to set the left bounds of the permissible neoliberal discourse, as it was still fixed in an evaluative and monitorial register concerned as it was with the question of whether or not teachers are to blame for problems in the educational domain.

Identifying Frames in the Dominant News Coverage

In extracting sources for this investigation, I queried news articles related to the teachers' uprising in Chicago in 2012 and the multi-state uprising in 2018. For the former, I searched for articles dated between September 1, 2012 and December 31, 2012 containing the words "Chicago teachers" in the four largest national newspapers by circulation: The New York Times, The Washington Post, USA Today, and The Wall Street Journal. I included both news articles and op-eds in my study but excluded blogs from the web-only editions of the papers. For the 2018 multi-state teacher uprising, I selected articles in the same publications dating from January 1, 2018 to May 31st, 2018, based on a search query for at least two of the following words "teachers, movement, strike, and protest." Once again, I included both news articles and op-eds but excluded blogs in the web-only editions of the papers. In both cases, I arrived at the date range based on the frequency of relevant articles. While local coverage leading up to the 2012 CTU strike was abundant through the summer of that year, national publications did not take notice until September. Meanwhile, analyses about its impact began to taper off toward the end of December. Likewise, murmurs of teacher discontent in 2018 began in early January and slowly tapered off by May of that year.

I began with an initial screening of articles clipped using an online search engine through the databases of the publications culled in the above process. First, I sorted articles by whether the treatment of teachers was negative, positive, or neutral. I then went back through each pile and asked myself what it was about each article that led me to render that initial judgment: what words, terminology, or overall tone led me to categorize each in those ways. I then inductively devised a coding scheme based upon these tendencies and used them to describe four dominant frames described below. In employing Tuchman's (1978) notion of a frame that organizes an attitude into "everyday reality," I sought to illustrate how certain viewpoints about education, teachers, and their movements were naturalized in the coverage.

The frames were determined by the preponderance of associated code words throughout the article. In cases where multiple frames were identified with an article, I gave preference to the frame established closest to the lead paragraph, i.e. the one that established the overarching attitude of the article. In this manner, I adhered to Chong and Druckman's (2007) conception of a frame being determined by both the values articulated in an article as well as the salience given to them. Specifically, they hold that frames are activated through attitude structures, which, among other things, are built upon considerations such as availability and accessibility (Chong & Druckman, 2007). In other words, for a frame to be salient, it must be something that the public has been repeatedly exposed to. In relation to the critical theory used as the framework of this study, I am arguing that these frames emerge out of common themes and tropes circulated by elite sectors of society, i.e. Hall's (2013) "primary definers." Journalists and their readership will almost unconsciously attach themselves to these attitudes, and their undergirding logics, because they have been so successfully disseminated for so long as part of the forty-year-long neoliberal project.

I ultimately found four dominant frames: two from the list of articles I deemed "negative," and one each from the "positive" and "neutral" piles. Among negative articles, I identified two frames, which I called the "Strict Father Frame" and the "Teacher vs. the People Frame." Meanwhile, neutral articles tended to fall into what I called the "War Frame." Lastly, the positive articles almost exclusively adhered to the "Savage Inequalities Frame." A more detailed description of each of these frames follows.

The first negative frame I identified portrays teachers variously as selfish, childish, and undisciplined. I label this one the "Strict Father Frame," following Lakoff's (2004) conception of the conservative ethos that extols discipline as the highest virtue in the formation of children. Regarding how this ethos informs certain aspects of neoliberal education policy, such as the advocacy of school vouchers, he says:

> Because immoral, undisciplined children can lead moral, disciplined children astray, parents should be able to choose to which school they send their children. Government funding should be taken from public schools and given to parents in the form of vouchers. This will help wealthier (more disciplined and moral) citizens send their children to private or religious schools that teach conservative values and impose appropriate discipline. (pp. 83–84)

The same logic largely animates the charter school movement, in addition to the related pedagogy of test-taking that undergirds neoliberal reforms. This rationale sees underperforming, undisciplined teachers as responsible for the perceived crisis of education, and the associated frame tends to exaggerate the effect that these teachers have on the overall state of education in this country. Poor performance by pupils is attributed to poor teachers, rather than any other factor that might have an impact on student performance.

I also categorized articles that placed disproportionate emphasis on economic realities within the domain of the "Strict Father" frame, owing to the fact that the overarching tenor remains one of discipline. As Apple (1986, 1995) argues, one of the fundamental disciplinary mechanisms of the neoliberal economy is its tendency to displace economic problems to other realms, most notably the educational system, which has the effect of blaming teachers for conditions largely out of their control. In my view, the other side of the coin of this tendency is singling education out for cuts when there is an economic downturn and concomitant drying of public coffers, rather than any of a number of other programs (or by asking the wealthy to pay more in taxes in order to cover budgetary shortfalls).

The second negative frame pits teachers against the society that they are inconveniencing because of the strike: be it students missing class or parents scrambling to find babysitters. I call it the "Teachers vs the

People" frame, as it makes teachers out to be selfishly pursuing their own interests at the expense of the body politic.

The third frame tends to read in a typically neutral, dispassionate journalistic tone.

Nonetheless, I argue that it trivializes the teachers' movements by placing the emphasis on political dynamics. This "War Frame" pits teachers against the major political leaders in the jurisdictions that the movements are operating in, such as the CTU vs Rahm Emanuel in 2012, which was the most pronounced political war frame in the coverage inspected in this investigation, owing in large part to the combative personalities of both Emanuel and then-CTU president Karen Lewis.

While this coverage occasionally sympathizes with teachers, I contend that it, nonetheless, tends to undermine their cause by taking the focus away from the issues being raised. Rather than framing the teachers as fighting for the interest of students and for the improvement of educational standards that would benefit the whole of society, this frame generally paints teachers as self-interested actors doing battle with other self-interested actors.

The fourth frame is the most sympathetic one toward the teachers' movements, insofar as it provides socioeconomic context. I call it the "Savage Inequalities Frame," in a nod to Kozol's (1991) work charting the inequities across school districts, particularly between predominantly white suburban districts and predominantly minority urban districts. This frame acknowledges that there are, indeed, social forces beyond teachers' control impacting student performance. Among the major national dailies, the Washington Post engaged this frame most often for the 2012 strike, owing in large part to having a dedicated education reporter, Valerie Strauss, who frequently wrote critically of the high-stakes testing regimen effected by the neoliberal reforms.

Nonetheless, my contention is that this frame, while more sympathetic toward teachers, does not effectively challenge the logics that have animated the neoliberal reform movement. Instead, it tends to incorporate the narrative about education being in crisis that has historically been used to justify neoliberal reforms, as discussed in Chapter 3 (Goldstein, 2014). The underlying logic here is that the duty of schools is to create productive workers for a dynamic economy. By extension, this logic sees economic productivity as inextricably tied to academic achievement. Individual economic success is seen as being a reflection of personal scholastic achievement, and, likewise, the obverse condition is held to be true: that is, economic problems across society are a sign that educational systems are failing (Goldstein, 2014).

In short, I hold that the "savage inequalities" frame, rather than breaking with the hegemonic view of education, instead sets its left boundary. While it recognizes that education systems operate inside of larger social systems, and that teachers cannot be held solely accountable for the struggles of their students, it continues to operate within the "education in crisis" paradigm and internalizes its instrumentalist logic, insofar as it does not generally question the notion that schools should be serving the market first and foremost. In this respect, it is illustrative of the deep contradictions of the liberal standpoint, which holds that, on the one hand, education suffers from injustices created by unrestrained market logics and, on the other hand, it must be fixed in order that it better serve the market.

A Shift to the Left Bounds of the Neoliberal Paradigm

The results of the frame analysis are tallied in Table 7.1 and 7.2 below for the 2012 CTU strike and 2018 strike wave, respectively. The two charts list the number of articles employing each of the frames delineated above, laid out from left to right as a reflection of the general political attitude of each frame: from the left bounds of the "Savage Inequalities" frame to the most overtly hostile frames: the "Teachers vs. the People" frame and the "Strict Father" frame.

The "War Frame" was the most immediately identifiable frame with its associated code words evoking fighting words of various sorts: battle,

Table 7.1 Distribution of Framing Categories in Articles Inspected During the 2012 CTU Strike

2012 CTU Wave	Strict Father	Teachers vs The People	War Frame	Savage Inequalities	None of the above
WaPo	11	6	14	11	4
NYT	5	5	16	5	3
USA Today	0	3	3	0	1
WSJ	10	5	19	0	4

Table 7.2 Distribution of Framing Categories in Articles Inspected During the 2018 Strike Wave

2018 Strike Wave	Strict Father	Teachers vs the People	War Frame	Savage Inequalities	None of the Above
WaPo	5	0	12	11	4
NYT	1	0	11	19	4
USA Today	1	0	1	2	0
WSJ	2	7	4	2	3

brawl, clash, conflict, showdown, confrontation, and the like. Here is a representative snippet from the September 27, 2012 Washington Post:

> The strike attracted national attention because the battle was over education reforms that mirrored conflicts taking place around the country and also because Emanuel, a prominent Democrat and President Obama's former chief of staff, was brawling with organized labor, a key constituency that Democrats need in the coming presidential election. (Layton, 2012)

At times, the word "war" itself was actually employed in order to delineate larger political implications of the strike, as in this paragraph (one down from the lead) in the September 12, 2012 edition of the New York Times:

> The strike pits several core components of the Democratic coalition against one another: The teachers' union and much of organized labor are on a war footing against Rahm Emanuel, Chicago's Democratic mayor and Mr. Obama's chief of staff. What is more, the strike pits organized labor against myriad wealthy liberals– vital donors to Democratic coffers - many of whom contribute heavily to efforts to finance charter schools and weaken teachers' unions. (Greenhouse, 2012)

This analysis of the political fault lines is arguably appropriate in coverage of the strike, though positioning the analysis toward the top of the article serves to minimize the issues animating the union movement, making it seem as if the teachers' "war footing" is mostly political theater. This playing to the news value of "conflict" also leads to a tendency to overdramatize the narrative. Take this lead from the September 19, 2012 edition of the New York Times exemplifies:

> The Chicago Teachers Union agreed on Tuesday to end its strike in the nation's third-largest school system, allowing 350,000 children to return to classes on Wednesday and bringing to a close, at least for now, a tense standoff over issues like teacher evaluation and job security that upended this city for more than a week. (Davey & Yaccino, 2012)

The notion that the nation's third-largest city was "upended" by the strike is probably a hyperbolic treatment of the political drama. This coverage also veers into the "Teacher vs. the People" frame, as it leaves the impression of the union gratuitously creating turmoil.

Treating the teachers as unprovoked disruptors was, indeed, the defining tendency of the "Teachers vs the People" frame. These usually came in the form of op-eds, such as this lead paragraph from Joe Nocera (2012), a business journalist opining on education matters: "No matter how quickly the Chicago teachers' strike ends, whether it is this afternoon or two months from now, it's not going to end well for the city's public school students." Joseph Epstein (2012), writing for the Wall Street Journal, concurs: "Whichever way the Chicago teachers strike ends, one may be fairly certain that the children of Chicago will not win." The code words include descriptions of students losing, being hurt, or being unfairly inconvenienced or disadvantaged by the strike.

Alternatively, the papers provide an anecdote highlighting the purported injury done to students, such as a Washington Post article quoting a mother who said she had to send her son 15 miles away each weekday to a cousin's house "so he wouldn't be left unsupervised in a neighborhood known for violent crime and gangs." While there was undoubtedly some hardship on the part of parents having to arrange care for their children, it is misleading to provide anecdotes like this one without also noting that the vast majority of parents supported the strike (Uetricht, 2014), and that the CTU made much effort to organize community members in the lead-up to the work stoppage, viewing their efforts, as they did, as part of a broader social movement (Ashby & Bruno, 2016; Brogan, 2014). In a similarly framed article in the September 17, 2012 Wall Street Journal, the authors found a rally with "more than 20 parents gathered... to protest the teachers strike. Some carried signs that said: '350,000 CPS hostages! Let our children learn'" (Porter & Nicas, 2012). A group of twenty people on a street corner was deemed newsworthy enough to run with this hostile frame. Nonetheless, that was more than they needed to claim frustration on the part of parents in other articles, such as the May 1, 2018 piece updating on the strike in Arizona, which led with, "Arizona parents kept scrambling to find alternative arrangements for their children as the state faced a fourth day of teacher walkouts Tuesday" (Hobbs & Hackman, 2018, p. A3). No evidence outside of a single anecdote is provided to corroborate this lead, the spirit of which is ultimately contradicted through a corrective final paragraph, declaring: "Many parents have spoken out in support of teachers, though some acknowledge the inconvenience of needing alternative child-care plans" (Hobbs & Hackman, 2018, p. A3).

This frame often overlapped with the "strict father" frame insofar as it involved chastising teachers for behavior deemed out of acceptable bounds. The Wall Street Journal spent the greatest percentage of its coverage of the teachers' movement operating in this frame, usually by taking a disciplinary tone discussing the perceived waste in education spending. The lead from this op-ed in the September 21, 2012 Wall Street Journal exemplifies this tendency:

> Now that Chicago's children have returned to not learning in school, we can all move on to the next crisis in Illinois public finance: unfunded public pensions. Readers who live in the other 49 states will be pleased to learn that Governor Pat Quinn's 2012 budget proposal already floated the idea of a federal guarantee of its pension debt. Think Germany and Eurobonds for Greece, Italy and Spain.
> Thank you for sharing, Governor.
> Sooner or later, we knew it would come to this since the Democrats who are running Illinois into the ground can't bring themselves to oppose union demands. Illinois now has some $8 billion in current debts outstanding and taxpayers are on the hook for more than $200 billion in unfunded retirement costs for government workers. By some estimates, the system could be the first in the nation to go broke, as early as 2018. (An Illinois Pension Bailout?, 2012)

This frame is more determined by tone than in specific code words: a disciplinary tone scolding teachers for being out of line and public officials for not taking them to task. Together, they are to blame for budget shortfalls, and surely not the reckless, imprudent investors that threw the country into financial crisis in 2007–2008, thus precipitating the ongoing public budget problems. In other words, the "Strict Father" frame is generally short on context and history, though it is occasionally long on smugness, as evinced by Amanda Ripley's op-ed in the September 15,

2012 Wall Street Journal, where she declares, "Many countries have revolutionized their education systems in recent years, but not one of them has done it through strikes, walkouts or righteous indignation" (Ripley, 2012).

The frame that is most sympathetic to the teachers' cause, wherein student performance is treated as being a function of broader socioeconomic issues, is the "Savage Inequalities" frame. Among the major national daily papers, the Washington Post most often employed it, owing largely to the presence of dedicated educational reporter Valerie Strauss, as well as liberal columnist Eugene Robinson. The latter wrote one of the best examples of an op-ed from this perspective in the September 18, 2012 edition:

> It is reasonable to hold teachers accountable for their performance. But it is not reasonable – or, in the end, productive – to hold them accountable for factors that lie far beyond their control. It is fair to insist that teachers approach their jobs with the assumption that every child, rich or poor, can succeed. It is not fair to expect teachers to correct all the imbalances and remedy all the pathologies that result from growing inequality in society. You didn't see any of this reality in "Waiting for Superman," the 2010 documentary that argued we should "solve" the education crisis by establishing more charter schools and, of course, stomping the teachers' unions. You won't see it later this month in "Won't Back Down," starring Viola Davis and Maggie Gyllenhaal, which argues for "parent trigger" laws designed to produce yet more charter schools and yet more teacher-bashing. (Robinson, 2012).

This piece embodies the "savage inequalities" frame insofar as it criticizes the "teacher bashing" present in more conservative framings of the teachers' movement, while, nonetheless, operating within the discursive bounds of the neoliberal paradigm by employing terminology about an "education crisis." This "crisis" is not contextualized as part of a broader political project of eviscerating public institutions under the guise of austerity, nor is the "inequality" mentioned placed in the context of that intentional political project. The impression left by this treatment is that these are "social ills": problems of a sort that need to be addressed through policy prescriptions (just not those prescriptions advocated by reformers). A more radical rendering would be that inequality is a natural feature of the existing social order—one that would manifest in education just as readily as anywhere else—and that addressing inequalities both inside and outside of the education system requires a restructuring of that social order. I would argue that the CTU, by organizing outside of its membership ranks within the broader communities in which it operates (Brogan, 2014; Uetricht, 2014), embraces a radical vision not captured by the left liberal bounds of the "Savage Inequalities" frame.

Another example of this approach was glimpsed in the pages of the Washington Post during the 2018 strike wave in an op-ed by Paul Waldman, writing:

> There's a revolt beginning among the nation's schoolteachers, one that could well pick up momentum and spread around the country. Or it might be more properly understood as a revolt among teachers in states governed by Republicans…What we're seeing is an indictment of the Republican model of taxation, spending and governance. Oklahoma's schools and educators have endured some of the steepest cuts in education in the last decade, reductions that are evident in dwindling supplies, aging textbooks and the pay stubs of teachers. Before last week, state lawmakers have not raised the minimum salary for teachers in a decade, making them among the worst paid in the nation. (Waldman, 2018)

Once again, the left boundary of the neoliberal paradigm criticizes its right flank, with the author attributing problems in education to Republican governance, papering over the fact that the strike wave began in a solidly Democratic city and state in Chicago in 2012, and the reform movement that has roused teachers throughout the country has been promulgated by both parties. While Republicans have undoubtedly gone further in their gutting of the public sector, and probably merit more attention, the reality is that neoliberal logics have been hegemonic within both major political parties over much of the last forty years. Moreover, the more recent wave of teacher uprisings was not limited to the "red states" that saw walkouts in the spring in 2018, but also includes subsequent actions taken in Democratic locales, such as Los Angeles, Denver, and Oakland (not to mention Chicago yet again).

The forces teachers are facing in red states and blue cities have grown similar in recent years, due to the increasing nationalization of education policy. While traditionally the domain of states and local jurisdictions, education become more and more uniform throughout the country, owing to the sophistication and power of neoliberal reformers in organizing their efforts. A recent study by Reckhow et al (2019) found that this influence has been able to effectively undermine teachers' union powers in the five cities they inspected: Bridgeport, Conn.; Denver; New Orleans; Indianapolis; and Los Angeles. In looking at the impact of 132 "large national donors" in school board elections in these cities, they found:

> In four of the five cities we studied, the education reform organizations and independent expenditure committees outspent teacher unions. These trends have continued in Los Angeles through the most recent election cycle. In 2017, Los Angeles held a school board election that spent more campaign funds than ever had been spent in the United States. And two-thirds of that spending came from organizations supporting charter expansion.
> The federal campaign contributions of these large national donors show that they are mostly Democrats. That fact reveals sharp divisions within the Democratic Party over education policy. (para. 11)

The fight for teachers is being waged not only against their traditional opponents, the Republicans, but also against Democrats that have embraced neoliberal reforms. The fact that the "savage inequalities" frame generally does not acknowledge the bipartisan nature of this assault on teachers places severe limitations on its ability to capture the larger social forces at work behind the reform movement in American education.

Nonetheless, this framing is more sympathetic toward teachers in general, and it is significant that reportage shifted more in its direction during the 2018 uprising: reflective, I would argue, of the fact that teachers successfully pushed the discourse on education in a more critical direction.

This shift largely came at the expense of the "Teachers vs the People" frame, which virtually vanished from view. In fact, when certain politicians took to engaging this frame themselves, accusing teachers of compromising the interests of the general public, much of the reportage on their remarks was sympathetic to teachers. The most notable example came in response to former Kentucky Governor Matt Bevin's admonishing of teachers for their walkout, when he accused them of endangering student welfare by declaring: "I guarantee you somewhere in Kentucky today a child was sexually assaulted that was left at home because there was nobody there to watch them." The most prominent newspaper in the state, the Louisville Courier-Journal, responded with an article by their dedicated education reporter, Mandy McLaren, highlighting the disgust felt by members of the public. Her article led with:

Republican Gov. Matt Bevin's "guarantee" that a teacher protest led to a child being sexually abused somewhere in Kentucky added to the outrage that many educators say they have been feeling for months.
"For the governor of the state of Kentucky to come out and basically say teachers are responsible for children being molested — are you serious?" said J.P. LaVertu, a Shelby County teacher. "He's a disgrace to our state." Bevin's comments, which he made to reporters Friday evening, have been widely condemned by educators and scorned by members of both parties.

For the sake of newsworthiness, the article places an emphasis on conflict, and thus falls under a variant of the "War Frame," though in a much more sympathetic light for teachers, which was part of a broader trend with that frame in 2018. By rendering the "War Frame" one of a broad-based popular movement taking on individual politicians, the coverage tended to be much more favorable to teachers, compared to 2012, when the frame focused on the dueling personalities of former Chicago Mayor Rahm Emanuel and former CTU President Karen Lewis.

Meanwhile, there was far more coverage falling under the "savage inequalities" frame at the national level. In this case, the frame tended to focus on disparities between the states wherein actions took place and the national average. These reports provided data discussing how these states were all at or near the bottom nationally in per-pupil student funding and teacher pay. The New York Times especially shifted its focus from "war frame" coverage to "savage inequalities." While it is likely that part of this shift is attributable to the lack of high-profile political actors to depict as being at war with each other, I hold that much of it has to do with a far more favorable environment for teachers to get their word across.

The difference in 2018 was that a broad-based national movement was underway, leading to more receptivity on the part of news media outlets to teachers' demands. Rather than one union engaging in battle with a mayor viewed favorably by the political and media establishments, teachers were now taking action in cities and towns across several different states. The effect of this was to have news media view this as a bona fide social movement rather than an isolated union action: giving them what Benford and Snow (2000) describe as the power of "signifying" agents. The teachers had effectively entered into the "contested realm of media discourse in which struggles over meaning and interpretation are central" (Gamson & Wolfseld, 1993, p. 119). Their collective action frame now had influence over the dominant news frames employed by major national newspapers.

Moreover, the 2018 movement has more institutional weight to it. Amenta et al.'s (2012) work on news framing of social movements demonstrates the importance of institutional actors as providing legitimacy. While unions were involved in both rounds of teacher actions, the CTU strike of 2012 involved a newly elected leadership that was challenging established hegemonic thinking about the role of the union in the city, and thus probably did not carry the same institutional weight at the time. However, in 2018, when teachers were taking action in unison throughout the country, the institutional factor held greater sway, despite those actions often being taken outside of formal union channels (the sheer breadth of the movement infused it with institutional legitimacy).

Nonetheless, I contend that even these more sympathetic, liberal portrayals fail to capture the underlying challenge to neoliberal pedagogy posed by these teachers. While the uprising of 2018 made it easy to portray the movement as one of teachers taking on their states' Republican lawmakers, the larger story undermines that narrative when one considers the many "blue cities" that have seen teacher actions since then. Moreover, while the "Savage Inequalities" frame recognizes the prevalence of inequities in this country's school systems, it rarely probes the underlying causes of their existence. The larger social forces, most notably the forty-year neoliberal project of elite retrenchment focused on eviscerating the public sector, are rarely mentioned in any coverage. The result is to leave the impression that inequality is some mysterious social ill: a disease of the social fabric, rather than the natural result of an intentional social and political project.

In short, this relatively sympathetic frame tends to see problems of education as isolated from other societal problems. In contrast, the conservative rendering (the right bounds of the neoliberal discourse) views education as the *cause* rather than a *reflection* of a larger social malaise. Apple (1996) explains:

> The political Right in the United States has been very successful in mobilizing support against the educational system and its employees, often exporting the crisis in the economy to the schools. Thus, one of its major achievements has been to shift the blame for unemployment and underemployment, for the loss of economic competitiveness, and for the supposed breakdown of "traditional" values and standards in the family, education,

and paid and unpaid workplaces, from the economic, cultural, and social policies and effects of dominant groups to the school and other public agencies. (p. 28)

The effect of this successful project has been to structure the discourse around education in such a way that educators are placed on the defensive. The dominant question animating this discourse is "Are teachers to blame for myriad social and economic problems? Yes or no?" The conservative rendering answers "yes," and the liberal rendering answers "no"; meanwhile, the discursive bounds limit any possibility of suggesting that the direction of causality should be reversed, i.e. that social and economic structures are to blame for dysfunction within the educational system. With this said, it is now worth revisiting the example above from Eugene Robinson's piece in the Washington Post, where he says, "It is not fair to expect teachers to correct all the imbalances and remedy all the pathologies that result from growing inequality in society." His posture here is defensive: He is being sympathetic toward teachers by suggesting that problems entirely out of their control are not their fault. A more critical approach, breaking free of the confines of neoliberal discourse, would be to note that not only are teachers not the villains in this saga, but they are actually victims of the larger problem of an unequal society in which the public sector—especially the educational sector—has been singled out for austerity and monitorial mechanisms of control.

Finally Some Discussion of Issues

This snapshot of news framing around the two teacher strike waves—in 2012 and 2018—is instructive in demonstrating the range of permissible debate on the role of education in society and how the center of gravity can change based on prevailing social dynamics. Much of the news coverage, especially in 2012, was devoid of serious discussion of issues, instead focusing on the political battles between the two key figures in Chicago: then-Mayor Rahm Emanuel and then-CTU President Karen Lewis. Other coverage, especially in op-eds, would scold teachers for inconveniencing parents by striking (despite polls showing overwhelming support for teachers on the part of the public). And, when issues were discussed, it tended to be in a trivializing way, i.e. focusing narrowly on teacher pay and education spending, while ignoring the myriad other issues teachers raised.

Nonetheless, the 2018 coverage did at least make mention of those few issues, while casting teachers in a significantly more positive light. As already mentioned, this shift was, in part, informed by the fact that the 2018 uprising was far more widespread, so it could not be so easily dismissed as an isolated event. In this case, the news media conceded to a nominally critical view that had become popular with the public. This is consistent with how counterhegemonic views are occasionally allowed to hold sway, albeit in very limited ways. Kumar (2007) relates:

> Critical views do find a space in the media through many avenues, even when there is not significant conflict among various social groups. However, these expressions of dissent are not truly significant, because they typically do not set the terms of discussion or impact how the news is gathered, packaged, and sold to the public. (p. 50)

So, while the 2018 coverage became more sympathetic toward striking teachers, reflective of the success of teachers in using their "signifying power" to shift news media discourse on the role of education in society, this shift did not effectively break with the neoliberal paradigm. The prevailing discourse largely stuck within the bounds set by the evaluative/monitorial register of neoliberalism. The effect of that register on news framing has been to pose the question about whether or not teachers are to blame for larger societal ills, rather than locating those ills in the concerted actions of an elite waging a forty-year counteroffensive on poor and working people.

Nonetheless, the existence of some evidence of a discursive shift in the way teachers were portrayed in these leading news publications is significant. The fact that coverage tended to be a bit more sympathetic demonstrates the value of the communicative and discursive interventions that teacher activists have undertaken in their tactical shift away from traditional union organizing. While the scope of this study is far too limited to make sweeping conclusions about the interplay between social media discourses and establishment news frames, it is safe to say that there would not have been so much ink spent in 2018 on the problems and injustices in American education had these teachers not taken action and initiated discourses to that effect. By stepping out of the narrow bounds of the bargaining room and into the (digital and literal) streets, teacher activists created a spectacle that even elite news media could not ignore.

References

Amenta, E., Caren, N., & Stobaugh, J. (2012). Political reform and the historical trajectories of U.S. social movements in the twentieth century. *Social Forces, 90*(4), 1073–1100.

An Illinois pension bailout? Governor Quinn wants you to guarantee his state's pensions. (2012, September 20). *The Wall Street Journal.* Retrieved from www.wsj.com

Apple, M. (1986). *Teachers and texts: A political economy of class and gender relations in education.* Routledge.

Apple, M. (1995). *Education and power* (2nd ed.). Routledge.

Apple, M. (1996). *Cultural politics and education.* Teachers College Press.

Ashby, S., & Bruno, R. (2016). *A fight for the soul of public education: The story of the Chicago teachers strike.* Cornell University Press.

Ayers, W. (2001). A Teacher ain't nothin' but a hero: Teachers and teaching in film. In P. B. Joseph & G. Burnaford (Eds.), *Images of Schoolteachers in America* (pp. 201–210). Lawrence Erlbaum Associates.

Benford, R., & Snow, D. (2000). Framing processes and social movements: An overview and assessment. *Annual Review of Sociology, 26*(2000), 611–639.

Brogan, P. (2014). Getting to the CORE of the Chicago Teachers' Union transformation. *Studies in Social Justice, 8*(2), 145–164.

Chong, D., & Druckman, J. N. (2007). A theory of framing and opinion formation in competitive elite environments. *Journal of Communication, 57*(1), 99–118.

Davey, M., & Yaccino, S. (2012, September 19). Teachers end Chicago strike on second try. *The New York Times*, p. 1.

Epstein, J. (2012, September 12). *Striking Teachers, Divided Antipathies.* Retrieved from, https://www.washingtonpost.com

Gamson, W., & Wolfsfeld, G. (1993). Movements and media as interacting systems. *The Annals of the American Academy of Political and Social Science, 528*, 114–125.

Goldstein, D. (2014). *The teacher wars: A history of America's most embattled profession.* Doubleday.

Greenhouse, S. (2012, September 13). Labor fight poses risks to coalition for Obama. *The New York Times*, p. 22.

Hall, S. (2013). *Policing the crisis: Mugging, the state, and law and order* (2nd ed.). Palgrave Macmillan.

Herman, E. S., & Chomsky, N. (1988). *Manufacturing consent: The political economy of the mass media.* Pantheon Books.

Hobbs, T., & Hackman, M. (2018, May 1). Arizona teacher walkout drags on. *The Wall Street Journal*, A3.

Kantor, K., Kantor, N. L., Kantor, J., Eaton, M., & Kantor, B. (2001). "I will not expose the ignorance of the faculty": The Simpsons as school satire. In P.

B. Joseph & G. Burnaford (Eds.), *Images of Schoolteachers in America* (2nd ed., pp. 185–200). Lawrence Erlbaum Associates.

Kumar, D. (2007). *Outside the box: Corporate media, globalization, and the UPS strike*. University of Illinois Press.

Lakoff, G. (2004). *Don't think of an elephant! Know your values and frame the debate: The essential guide for progressives*. Chelsea Green Pub. Co.

Layton, L. (2012, September 27). Chicago teachers reach tentative deal with Emanuel, ending five-day strike. *Washington Post*. Retrieved from, https://www.washingtonpost.com

Lippmann, W. (1922). *Public opinion*. Harcourt.

Nocera, J. (2012, September 18). How to fix the schools. *The New York Times*, p. 25.

Porter, C., & Nicas, J. (2012, September 17). Parents, and yes, students, tiring of closed schools. *The New York Times*. Retrieved from, https://www.nytimes.com

Reckhow, S., Jacobsen, R., & Henig, J. (2019, March 8). Why are teachers protesting in 'blue' cities? *Washington Post*, Retrieved from, https://www.washingtonpost.com

Ripley, A. (2012, September 15). Training teachers to embrace reform—Chicago-style war with unions is the past. *The Wall Street Journal*, C2.

Robinson, E. (2012, September 18). Standing up for teachers; The classroom isn't the only problem in the nation's education gap. *The Washington Post*. Retrieved from, https://www.washingtonpost.com

Tuchman, G. (1978). *Making news*. Free Press.

Uetricht, M. (2014). *Strike for America*. Verso.

Waldman, P. (2018, April 2). Teachers are walking out in multiple states. Blame GOP economics. *The Washington Post*. Retrieved from, https://www.washingtonpost.com

CHAPTER 8

Conclusion: Teacher Activism in Reactionary Times

Abstract This chapter returns to the theoretical discussion in Chapter 4 about the relationship between ideology, power, discourses, and education. In that discussion, I argue that Althusser severely discounts the agency of educators. Teachers have been operating in conditions not of their own making, but that are, rather, the results of structural forces often beyond their own control. But within that architecture—the educational apparatus—they have a good deal of power, which explains how they have been able to organize movements of resistance to the attacks waged by elite reformers. Likewise, they have had to negotiate with an elite news media that has set restrictive boundaries on the debate around education policy. And yet, through their organizing, teachers have been able to shift the bounds of that debate in a more favorable direction.

Keywords Education and society · Education discourses · Teacher power · Critical pedagogy

Neoliberal ideology promotes notions of "freedom" and "flexibility" as the ultimate virtues, advocating a removal of any barriers to realizing these ends. However, this has not translated into protecting the freedom of educators on matters of pedagogy and curriculum. This apparent contradiction is explained by the fact that neoliberal "freedom" is narrowly

© The Author(s), under exclusive license to Springer Nature Switzerland AG 2025
M. Reichel, *Teacher Power in the Digital Age*, Social Movements and Transformation, https://doi.org/10.1007/978-3-031-87191-7_8

bound up with aligning government policy to an idealized "free market." In this rendering, teachers are impeding students from realizing their full capacity to thrive in the global market economy, and, so, government intervention is necessary in order to "free" students from this restraint.

This discourse has not only effectively served the purpose of legitimating neoliberal education reforms, but it has also prepared the ground for the reactionary attacks that have ensued since 2020 in municipalities and states throughout the country. In these largely Republican-led areas, policymakers have taken aim at diversity, equity, and inclusion (DEI) measures, as well as curriculum loosely lumped together under the moniker "critical race theory" (CRT). These attacks have exploited public anxieties over changing demographics and resentment over the popular movement that emerged in the summer of 2020 in response to the release of the gut-wrenching video showing George Floyd being killed by a Minnesota police officer. This mass display of cross-racial solidarity in opposition to police brutality sparked a response from far-right political leaders seeking to advance a white supremacist agenda of erasure in which pupils are denied access to truths about the history of repression and subjugation of non-white peoples in the United States (Hagopian, 2025).

This policing of what Hagopian (2025) terms "truthcrimes" is also designed to stoke fear and anxiety in a teaching corps that has been battered by decades of the neoliberal policies of control discussed throughout this book. The reactionary right desires a teaching corps that is too fearful to engage critical confrontation with the nation's legacy of structural racism, from slavery to Jim Crow to the contemporary carceral state. They know that teachers already fearing for their job security are less likely to defy laws governing curriculum, especially when these laws have emerged out of hot-blooded political rhetoric accusing them of indoctrinating youth with "radical ideas."

These accusations come against the backdrop of attacks aimed against students that participated in lawful protests against U.S. support of Israel's offensive on Gaza. These protests grew to include encampments at roughly 140 university campuses throughout the country, in what became one of the largest national protest movements against a foreign war in the country's history. Under the leadership of Marco Rubio, the State Department has weaponized its oversight of student visas to deny residency to graduate students that participated in protests or, in some cases, just voiced support for them. In one instance, immigration agents arrested Mahmoud Khalil, a graduate student who was among the leaders of Columbia University's student protest movement, ultimately sending him to a detention center in Louisiana, where he has been held without due process (which the Trump administration wrongly claims that visa holders are not entitled to). A Turkish graduate student at Tufts University, Rumeysa Ozturk, was sent to the same detention facility after having her student visa revoked for simply co-authoring a letter to the university president condemning his inaction on the Israeli offensive, despite a student senate resolution calling for university divestment. Several other students have also been detained for similar reasons, despite none of them having been in violation of any law. These arrests are the clearest sign yet of the administration's authoritarian impulse, and they are clearly designed to induce fear into young people about speaking out against injustices in the world.

At the same time, the Trump administration has revived a long-held Republican goal of dismantling the Department of Education. In an executive order signed on March 20, 2025, the president instructed his education secretary Linda McMahon to "take all necessary steps to facilitate the closure of the Department of Education and return authority over education to the States and local communities while ensuring the effective and uninterrupted delivery of services, programs, and benefits on which Americans rely" (Dipierro & Fensterwald, 2025). He had already halved the department's workforce of 4,100 as part of the broader cuts in government bureaucracy brought on by Elon Musk's "department of government efficiency" initiative. However, in reality, the move is less motivated by a desire to reduce costs and more by a desire to make it easier for states and municipalities to pursue the kinds of alternative school policies highlighted throughout this book. Public school advocate Guillermo Mayer makes this case succinctly: "While this order purports to reduce federal bureaucracy, it's part of a longer-term plan to eliminate federal oversight in education and give states free rein to redirect billions of dollars away from public schools and towards private school vouchers. The ultimate goal is to erode the public's trust in our system of public education" (Dipierro & Fensterwald, 2025).

It is in this populist rhetoric undermining teachers and education that one glimpses most vividly how these attacks on DEI and CRT are an outgrowth of the neoliberal policies that preceded them. While neoliberal reforms did not explicitly ban critical pedagogical methods or threaten the existing of the Department of Education, they devalued the teaching of subjects not narrowly focused on skill development that could be easily assessed on standardized tests. Neoliberal reformers have treated education like Freire's "banking model," in which skills and technical knowledge are deposited into subjects who deploy those resources in future careers. Those subjects that do not directly contribute to this market-oriented sense of value are seen as less worthwhile. This tendency has been exacerbated by a concomitant cut in funding of higher education, leading to increasing tuition costs for students, who resultantly see themselves as customers and education as a commodity. In this transactional view of education, critical pedagogies are especially viewed as a waste of time, or, worse yet, as "indoctrination."

In this context, right-wing politicians have seized on rising anti-establishment sentiment to cast teachers and university professors in these disciplines as "elitists" perpetuating a political agenda at the public's expense. This rhetoric has succeeded precisely because neoliberal reformers had already normalized the demonization of teachers and the belittling of education as a profession. They have also naturalized the neoliberal conceptualization of negative freedom. This is how Republican lawmakers in Florida could unironically name their anti-CRT legislation the "Individual Freedom Act." In their view, it is infringing on the "freedom" of white students to make them learn about systems of racism that undergird American history. The law states: "A person should not be instructed that he or she must feel guilt, anguish, or other forms of psychological distress for actions, in which he or she played no part, committed in the past by other members of the same race or sex" (FL SB 148).

If such rhetoric was coming from a small political fringe, it could be summarily dismissed as nonsense. Unfortunately, it is coming from an ideological current that has become dominant in the Republican Party and that enjoys widespread popular support, especially in so-called "red states."

In response, educators must recast themselves as servants of the people and allies of communities by embracing and expanding on the acts of radical pedagogy already present in their midst. Firstly, this means supporting initiatives by parents, teachers, and students in locales that have sought to mimic Florida's "anti-woke" agenda. For example, when Pennsylvania's Central York School Board banned over three hundred literary and artistic works dealing with themes of race and racism in August 2020, five concerned students mobilized a larger group to join them in bombarding the next board meeting with complaints about the new law. And they succeeded in convincing the board to change course. One of the organizers, Edha Gupta, declared: "Our voices are powerful enough to demand immediate action, and that is EXACTLY what took place tonight" (Hagopian, p. 166). It is important that political leaders and other members of society hear voices of dissent on these matters, making it clear that students do not feel victimized by their exposure to an antiracist pedagogy.

Secondly, this means engaging dialogic pedagogical methods in classroom instruction that encourage students to generate their own solutions to social problems. One such example is the "Teaching SNCC" lesson, referring to the Student Nonviolent Coordinating Committee, which was one of the most important groups at the forefront of the fight against Jim Crow era segregation laws. In this activity, students pretend to be organizers, deliberating in groups over questions like "Should SNCC prioritize voter registration or direct action?" and "Should SNCC welcome a thousand mostly white volunteers to Mississippi?" An activity of this nature stands in stark contrast to the "indoctrination" that reactionary politicians claim teachers to be engaged in. At the same time, it empowers students to feel in control of their own convictions and to be involved in conversations on important social problems (Hagopian, 2025).

Lastly, educational practitioners and institutions at all levels must embrace partnerships with community organizations to illustrate their commitment to the interests thereof. In this regard, they should follow the lead of the CTU and its work in building the Grassroots Education Movement (GEM), wherein teacher activists built connections with neighborhood groups around their common interest in protecting traditional public schools against the onslaught of neoliberal reforms. When the CTU took its members out on strike in 2012 and 2019, they enjoyed widespread public support, owing in large part to the fact that they meticulously cultivated these community alliances.

At the level of higher education, academics should try to replicate this alliance building through programs within the formal curriculum encouraging student work within the community. For example, a number of universities have public interest communication and journalism programs that forge alliances between their departments and community groups working in relevant areas. Through these programs, students obtain hands-on experience while learning about social issues and gaining the same sense affirmation that students experienced in the lessons on Jim Crow and segregation outlined above.

It is also important for formal organizing bodies to work together in coalition building. There has been some encouraging movement in that direction, with new leadership of the American Association of University Professors (AAUP) promising to take the body in a more combative direction. The recently elected president Todd Wolfson (my friend and dissertation advisor) has pushed to make the professional organization more overtly political and combative in fighting the extremism that has emerged in recent years, while also bringing the AAUP in closer coordination with the AFT (Quinn, 2024). Similarly, the CTU has sought to expand on its community-building practices by forging new labor alliances, most notably with the United Auto Workers (UAW). The CTU is joining them in a May Day planning activity designed to cement deeper ties in the future. Current CTU president Stacey Gates says: "Whether you are a parent on the West side of Chicago or you are a healthcare worker in York, Pennsylvania, we are all under the assault of billionaires and corporate elites who are dead set on upending our democracy" (Chicago Teachers' Union, 2025).

At the same time, leaders of universities and school districts should stand resolute in the face of reforms demanding a whitewashing of history. It is not an educator's job to make students feel better about atrocities committed in this country's past. Instead, it should be accepted that part of the maturation process is confronting unsettling facts about the world. Nonetheless, in the short term, it is understandable that some educators will feel pressured to conform to the mandates of "truthcrime" legislation due to fears of losing their jobs or other forms of retribution. It is undoubtedly challenging for teachers to face such a hostile political current that resents their work for contributing to the "woke"-ness of society.

However, as the history related in this book makes clear, teachers are unlikely to acquiesce without a fight. Over the last few decades, thousands of teachers throughout the country have stood up in the face of stagnant wages, decrepit working conditions, loss of hard-won autonomy, and the implementation of metric-driven mechanisms of control by political reformers. Moreover, they have done so despite severe legal and structural limitations. In some cases, they have gone on strike despite being barred from doing so, and, in other cases, they raised issues not technically permitted as part of the formal bargaining process.

Not only have they raised these various issues about education oversight, assessment, and spending models, but they have also pushed back on discourses that have disproportionately laid blame on educators for perceived failures of the nation's school systems. In this book, I have argued that this discursive intervention has been vital, because it contests the central neoliberal argument about the inherent failings of the public sector. Moreover, it does so in a core cultural institution involved in the reproduction and legitimation of the prevailing hegemonic order. Indeed, the importance of education as a cultural arena is precisely the reason that the radical right has singled out education policy as an area of emphasis with the current attacks on antiracist pedagogy. And it is also why neoliberal reformers previously engaged in fear mongering about a "crisis in education" that has put the "nation at risk." They understand that education policy is incredibly important in terms of how citizens perceive and make sense of the world they inhabit.

The difference between these elite reformers and teachers is that the latter are intimately connected to the communities they serve. In many smaller districts, teachers employed full-time in the local school have had every child in that community pass through their classroom. And they have usually interfaced with every parent and concerned community member during parent–teacher conferences and local school council meetings. It is no surprise, then, that teacher activists have enjoyed widespread public support in every location that they have gone on strike in recent years. Teacher power stems from these deep community ties and the vital public service that educators provide.

This power has been accentuated by the networking affordances of digital communication tools, especially during the 2018 rolling wave of walkouts and strikes. Nonetheless, social media is arguably less useful for these purposes these days, especially with the acquisition of Twitter (now X) by Elon Musk. There are also increasing concerns among activists about the nature of social media as a source of dataveillance in which users' behavioral data is the product used to generate profit for the platform users (Zuboff and Schwandt, 2019). Meanwhile, platform algorithms have increasingly been tailored narrowly for that purpose, which has caused political content to be de-prioritized, thus making it more difficult for activists to connect around common cause.

Nonetheless, the underlying technological affordances of the Internet still exist, even if they have been corrupted by corporate greed. There is the potential for the networking power of these technologies to manifest in robust social movements, despite current challenges. To that end, progressive political forces should advocate that existing platforms be subjected to a stricter regulatory regime characterized by algorithmic transparency and the mandate that space be preserved for public interest news and deliberation on important social issues, though achieving these goals is unlikely in the current political climate. What's more, existing networking tools can be appropriated by activist groups in creative ways, as Tiziana Bonini and Emiliano Trere (2024) document in their book *Algorithms of Resistance*. It is important that activists are aware of these issues of algorithmic governance and tactics that can be employed in working around the structural restraints that prevailing algorithmic systems pose on user activity, so that future movements are better equipped at navigating a media ecology in which surveillance capitalism is the organizing social logic.

In the meantime, it is clear that the "movements of the squares" wave of contestation has subsided, though it has left lasting impacts. First and foremost, these movements have collectively reshaped dominant political discourse to include topics of income and wealth inequality. For most of the neoliberal epoch, such issues were excluded from mainstream American political rhetoric. Likewise, "socialism" was once a dirty word, and now some of the most popular politicians at the national level attach this label to themselves, including Bernie Sanders and Alexandria Ocasio-Cortez. And the issues of racial reckoning raised by the Black Lives Matter movement have risen to the fore of the nation's discourse.

For its part, the teachers' movement has put education issues on the discursive agenda, while providing a model for teacher activists organizing in the future. They have also positioned themselves alongside communities fighting to save their schools and to stop the politics of "truthcrime" policing that has spread over the last five years. With the election of Donald Trump to a second term, the battle has become ever more fundamental, as progressive forces have to contend with the prospect of authoritarianism on top of all of the same issues they have been confronting throughout the neoliberal epoch. Now, more than ever, teachers must see themselves as heeding the call of American Federation of Teachers' founder Margaret Haley "to preserve and develop the democratic ideal" (Carter, 1990).

References

Bonini, T., & Trere, E. (2024). *Algorithms of resistance*. The MIT Press.

Carter, P. (1990). The social status of women teachers in the early twentieth century. In R. J. Altenbaugh (Ed.), *The teachers's voice: A social history of teaching in twentieth century America* (pp. 124–136).

Chicago Teachers' Union. (2025, March 19). *School Closures: Facts and statistics* [Press release]. https://www.ctulocal1.org/posts/ctu-kicks-off-two-day-meeting-with-national-grassroots-leaders-for-may-day-action/

Dipierro, A., & Fensterwald, J. (2025, March 20). *Trump signs executive order to dismantle Department of Education*. EdSource. https://edsource.org/2025/trump-signs-executive-order-to-dismantle-department-of-education/728843

Hagopian, J. (2025). *Teach truth: The struggle for antiracist education*. Haymarket Books.

Quinn, R. (2024). The AAUP's new president is not staying neutral. *Inside Higher Ed*. Retrieved from https://www.insidehighered.com/news/faculty-issues/academic-freedom/2024/10/30/aaups-new-president-not-staying-neutral

Zuboff, S., & Schwandt, K. (2019). *The age of surveillance capitalism: The fight for a human future at the new frontier of power*.

References

Altenbaugh, R. (1990). Teachers and the workplace. In R. J. Altenbaugh (Ed.), *The teachers's voice: A social history of teaching in twentieth century America* (pp. 124–136).

Althusser, L. (1971/2014). *On the reproduction of capitalism: Ideology and ideological state apparatuses*. Verso.

Amenta, E., Caren, N., & Stobaugh, J. (2012). Political reform and the historical trajectories of U.S. social movements in the twentieth century. *Social Forces, 90*(4), 1073–1100.

An Illinois pension bailout? Governor Quinn wants you to guarantee his state's pensions. (2012, September 20). *The Wall Street Journal*. Retrieved from www.wsj.com

Anderson, G. (2007). Media's impact on educational policies and practices: Political spectacle and social control. *Peabody Journal of Education, 82*(1), 103–120.

Apple, M. (1986). *Teachers and texts: A political economy of class and gender relations in education*. Routledge.

Apple, M. (1995). *Education and power* (2nd ed.). Routledge.

Apple, M. (1996). *Cultural politics and education*. Teachers College Press.

Apple, M. (2001). *Educating the right way: Markets, standards, god, and inequality*. Routledge.

Apple, M. (2006). *Educating the right way*. Routledge.

Apple, M. (2013). *Can education change society?* Routledge.

Apple, M., & Jungck, S. (1990). "You don't have to be a teacher to teach this unit": Teaching, technology and gender in the classroom. *American Educational Research Journal, 27*(2), 227–251.

Ashby, S., & Bruno, R. (2016). *A fight for the soul of public education: The story of the Chicago teachers strike*. Cornell University Press.

Ayers, W. (2001). A Teacher ain't nothin' but a hero: Teachers and teaching in film. In P. B. Joseph & G. Burnaford (Eds.), *Images of Schoolteachers in America* (pp. 201–210). Lawrence Erlbaum Associates.

Benford, R., & Snow, D. (2000). Framing processes and social movements: An overview and assessment. *Annual Review of Sociology, 26*(2000), 611–639.

Bennett, L., & Segerberg, A. (2013). *The logic of connective action: Digital media and the personalization of contentious politics*. Cambridge, University Press.

Bennett, W. L., & Graber, D. A. (2007). *News: The politics of illusion*. Pearson Longman.

Berliner, D., & Biddle, B. (1995). *The manufactured crisis: Myths, fraud and the attack on America's public schools*. Reading: Addison-Wesley.

Bernstein, B. (1990). *The structuring of pedagogic discourse*. Routledge.

Blanc, E. (2019). *Red state revolt*. Verso.

Bonini, T., & Trere, E. (2024). *Algorithms of resistance*. The MIT Press.

Bowles, S., & Gintis, H. (1976). *Schooling in capitalist America: Educational reform and the contradictions of economic life*. Basic Books.

Briffault, R. (2010). The Most popular tool: Tax increment financing and the political economy of local government. *The University of Chicago Law Review, 77*(1), 65–95.

Brogan, P. (2013). Education in global Chicago and the remaking of contemporary capitalism. *The Canadian Geographer/Le Geographe canadien* 2013, *57*(3), 303–310.

Brogan, P. (2014). Getting to the CORE of the Chicago Teachers' Union transformation. *Studies in Social Justice, 8*(2), 145–164.

Carnoy, M., & Levin, H. (1985). *Schooling and work in the democratic state*. Stanford University Press.

Carter, P. (1990). The social status of women teachers in the early twentieth century. In R. J. Altenbaugh (Ed.), *The teachers's voice: A social history of teaching in twentieth century America* (pp. 124–136).

Castells, M. (1989). *The informational city: Information technology, economic restructuring, and the urban-regional process*. Malden, MA: Blackwell.

Chadwick, A. (2013). *The hybrid media system*. Oxford University Press.

Chicago Teachers' Union. (2013, April 18). *Disproportionate number of teacher layoffs are black and latino*. [Press release]. https://www.ctulocal1.org/posts/school-closures-facts-and-statistics/

Chicago Teachers' Union. (2025, March 19). *School Closures: Facts and statistics* [Press release]. https://www.ctulocal1.org/posts/ctu-kicks-off-two-day-meeting-with-national-grassroots-leaders-for-may-day-action/

Chong, D., & Druckman, J. N. (2007). A theory of framing and opinion formation in competitive elite environments. *Journal of Communication, 57*(1), 99–118.
Cohen, J. (2010). Teachers in the news: A critical analysis of one US newspaper's discourse on education, 2006–2007. *Discourse: Studies in the Cultural Politics of Education, 31*(1), 105–119.
Dalla Costa, M., & James, S. (1975). *The power of women and the subversion of the community*. Falling Wall Press.
Darling-Hammond, L., & Skyes G. (2003). Wanted: A national teacher supply policy for education: The right way to meet the "highly qualified teacher" challenge. *Education Policy Analysis Archives, 11*(33).
Dean, J. (2019). Critique or collectivity? Communicative capitalism and the subject of politics. In D. Chandler & C. Fuchs (Eds.), *Digital objects digital subjects: Interdisciplinary perspectives on capitalism, labour and politics in the age of big data* (pp. 171–182). University of Westminster Press.
Davey, M., & Yaccino, S. (2012, September 19). Teachers end Chicago strike on second try. *The New York Times*, p. 1.
Delli Carpini, M. X., & Williams, B. A. (2001). Let us infotain you: Politics in the new media age. In W. L. Benne & R. M. Entman (Eds.), *Mediated politics: Communication in the future of democracy* (pp. 160–181). Cambridge University Press.
Desjardins, R. (2015). The Precarious role of education in identity and value formation processes: The Shift from state to market forces. *European Journal of Education, 50*(2), 134–146.
Dipierro, A., & Fensterwald, J. (March 20, 2025). *Trump signs executive order to dismantle Department of Education*. EdSource. https://edsource.org/2025/trump-signs-executive-order-to-dismantle-department-of-education/728843
Duda, J., & Small, J. (2021). Arizona Supreme Court sets the stage to overturn Prop 208 tax increase for school funding. *Arizona Mirror*. https://azmirror.com/2021/08/19/arizona-supreme-court-wont-block-prop-208-tax-increase-for-school-funding/
Dyer-Witheford, N. (1999). *Cyber-Marx: Cycles and circuits of struggle in high-technology capitalism*. University of Illinois Press.
Edling, S. (2014). Between curriculum complexity and stereotypes: Exploring stereotypes of teachers and education in media as a question of structural violence. *J. Curriculum Studies, 47*(3), 399–415.
Epstein, J. (2012, September 12). *Striking Teachers, Divided Antipathies*. Retrieved from, https://www.washingtonpost.com/
Engels, F., Morgan, L. H., & Engels, F. (1972). *The origin of the family, private property, and the state*. Pathfinder Press.
Fantasia, R., & Voss, K. (2004). *Hard work: Remaking the American labor movement*. University of California Press.

Farmer, S., & Poulos, C. (2015). Tax increment financing in Chicago, IL, Building neoliberal exclusion one school at a time. *Critical Sociology*, *41*(1), 153–171.
Federici, S. (2004). *Caliban and the witch*. Autonomedia.
Freire, P. (2018). *Pedagogy of the Oppressed*. Bloomsbury Publishing. (Original work published 1970).
Fortunati, L. (1995). *The arcane of reproduction: Housework, prostitution, labor and capital*. Autonomedia.
Fortunati, L. (2007). Immaterial labor and its machinization. *Ephemera*, *7*(1), 139–157.
Gamson, W., & Wolfsfeld, G. (1993). Movements and media as interacting systems. *The Annals of the American Academy of Political and Social Science*, *528*, 114–125.
Gandin, L., & Apple, M. (2002). Can education challenge neo-liberalism? The Citizen School and the struggle for democracy in Porto Alegre, Brazil. *Social Justice*, *29* (4 (90), 26–40.
Gerbaudo, P. (2012). *Tweets and the streets: Social media and contemporary activism*. Pluto Press.
Gerbaudo, P. (2017). *The mask and the flag: Populism, citizenism and global protest*. Oxford University Press.
Giddens, A. (1984). *The constitution of society: Outline of the theory of structuration*. University of California Press.
Gitlin, T. (2003). *The whole world is watching: Mass media in the making and unmaking of the new left*. The University of California Press.
Goldstein, D. (2014). *The teacher wars: A history of America's most embattled profession*. Doubleday.
Goldstein, R. (2011). Imaging the frame: Media representations of teachers, their unions, NCLB, and education reform. *Educational Policy*, *25*(4), 543–576.
Gramsci, A. (1971). In Q. Hoare, & G. Nowell-Smith (Eds.), *Selections from the prison notebooks of Antonio Gramsci*. International Publishers.
Greenhouse, S. (2012, September 13). Labor fight poses risks to coalition for Obama. *The New York Times*, p. 22.
Hagopian, J. (2025). *Teach truth: The struggle for antiracist education*. Haymarket Books.
Haley, Margaret. (1904, September 29). Why teachers should organize. *Journal of Education*, *60*(13), 215–216, 222.
Hall, S. (1985). Signification, representation, ideology: Althusser and the post-structuralist debates. *Critical Studies in Media Communication*, *2*(2), 91–114.
Hall, S. (1988). *The hard road to renewal: Thatcherism and the crisis of the left*. Verso.
Hall, S. (2013). *Policing the crisis: Mugging, the state, and law and order* (2nd ed.). Palgrave Macmillan.

Hall, S. (2016). *Cultural studies 1983: A theoretical history*. Duke University Press.
Hardt, M., & Negri, A. (2000). *Empire*. Harvard University Press.
Hardt, M., & Negri, A. (2004). *Multitude: War and democracy in the age of Empire*. The Penguin Press.
Hartman, A. (2003). The social production of American identity: Standardized testing reform in the United States. *Socialism and Democracy, 17*(2), 131–164.
Harvey, D. (2005). *A Brief history of neoliberalism*. Oxford University Press.
Herman, E. S., & Chomsky, N. (1988). *Manufacturing consent: The political economy of the mass media*. Pantheon Books.
Hobbs, T., & Hackman, M. (2018, May 1). Arizona teacher walkout drags on. *The Wall Street Journal*, A3.
Iyengar, S. (1991). *Is Anyone Responsible?: How television frames political issues*. University of Chicago Press.
Jameson, F. (1992). *Postmodernism, or, the Cultural Logic of Late Capitalism*. Duke University Press.
Jarrett, K. (2016). *Feminism, labour and digital media*. Routledge.
Kantor, K., Kantor, N. L., Kantor, J., Eaton, M., & Kantor, B. (2001). "I will not expose the ignorance of the faculty": The Simpsons as school satire. In P. B. Joseph & G. Burnaford (Eds.), *Images of Schoolteachers in America* (2nd ed., pp. 185–200). Lawrence Erlbaum Associates.
Kellner, D., & Share, J. (2007). Critical media literacy, democracy, and the reconstruction of education. In D. Macedo & S. R. Steinberg (Eds.), *Media literacy: A reader* (pp. 3–23). Peter Lang Publishing.
Klein, N. (2007). *The shock doctrine: The rise of disaster capitalism*. Picador.
Kumar, D. (2007). *Outside the box: Corporate media, globalization, and the UPS strike*. University of Illinois Press.
Lahann, R., & Reagan, E. M. (2011). Teach for America and the politics of progressive neoliberalism. *Teacher Education Quarterly, 38*(1), 7–27.
Lakoff, G. (2004). *Don't think of an elephant! Know your values and frame the debate: The essential guide for progressives*. Chelsea Green Pub. Co.
Layton, L. (2012, September 27). Chicago teachers reach tentative deal with Emanuel, ending five-day strike. *Washington Post*. Retrieved from, https://www.washingtonpost.com
Lipman, P. (2011). *The new political economy of urban education: Neoliberalism, race, and the right to the city*. Routledge.
Lippmann, W. (1922). *Public opinion*. Harcourt.
MacLean, N. (2017). *Democracy in chains: The deep history of the radical right's stealth plan for America*. Penguin.
Mandel, E. (1975). *Late capitalism*. Verso.

Marx, K. (1852). *The eighteenth Brumaire of Louis Bonaparte*. Marxists.org. Retrieved from, www.marxists.org

McAlevey, J. (2019, June 5). Traditional organizing is not failing. *Boston Review*. Retrieved from, www.bostonreview.net

McCartin, J., Sneiderman, M., & BP-Weeks, M. (2020). Combustible convergence: Bargaining for the common good and the #redfored uprisings of 2018. *Labor Studies Journal, 45*(1), 97–113.

McChesney, R. W., & Foster, J. (2014). Surveillance capitalism. *Monthly Review, 66*(3), 1–31.

McLaren, M., & Aulbach, L. (2018, April 13). Bevin: Children were sexually assaulted and tried drugs because teachers were protesting. *Louisville Courier-Journal*. https://www.courier-journal.com/story/news/politics/ky-legislature/2018/04/13/matt-bevin-kentucky-governor-children-sexually-assaulted-teacher-protests/516569002/

McNally, D. (2011). *Global slump: The economics and politics of crisis and resistance*. PM Press.

Moody, K. (1997). Towards an international social movement unionism. *New Left Review, 225*, 52–72.

Nocera, J. (2012, September 18). How to fix the schools. *The New York Times*, p. 25.

O' Cadiz, M., Wong P., Torres C. (1998). *Education and democracy: Paulo Freire, social movements, and educational reform in Sao Paolo*. Westview Press of local government. *The University of Chicago Law Review, 77*, 65.

Olssen, M. (1996). In defense of the welfare state and of publicly provided education. *Journal of Education, 11*(3), 337–362.

Parker, M., & Slaughter, J. (1988). *Choosing sides: Unions and the team concept*. South End Press.

Pickard, V. (2006). Assessing the radical democracy of Indymedia: Discursive, technical and institutional constructions. *Critical Studies in Media Communication, 23*(1), 19–38.

Piketty, T. (2014). *Capital in the twenty-first century*. Harvard University Press.

Polanyi, K. (1954). *The Great transformation*. Beacon Press.

Porter, C., & Nicas, J. (2012, September 17). Parents, and yes, students, tiring of closed schools. *The New York Times*. Retrieved from, https://www.nytimes.com

Putnam, R. D. (2000). *Bowling Alone: The Collapse and Revival of American Community*. Simon and Schuster, New York.

Quinn, R. (2024). The AAUP's new president is not staying neutral. *Inside Higher Ed*. Retrieved from https://www.insidehighered.com/news/faculty-issues/academic-freedom/2024/10/30/aaups-new-president-not-staying-neutral.

Reckhow, S., Jacobsen, R., & Henig, J. (2019, March 8). Why are teachers protesting in 'blue' cities? *Washington Post*, Retrieved from, https://www.washingtonpost.com

Reichel, M. (2018). Teachers' movements in the circuits of communication. *Critical Studies in Media Communication, 35*(5), 483–502.

Ripley, A. (2012, September 15). Training teachers to embrace reform—Chicago-style war with unions is the past. *The Wall Street Journal*, C2.

Robinson, E. (2012, September 18). Standing up for teachers; The classroom isn't the only problem in the nation's education gap. *The Washington Post*. Retrieved from, https://www.washingtonpost.com

Rooks, D., & Munoz, C. B. (2015). Brilliant, bored or badly behaved? Media coverage of the charter school debate in the United States. *Teachers College Record, 117*, 080302.

Sassen, S. (2001). *The global city: New York, London, Tokyo*. Princeton University Press.

Silver, B., & Slater, E. (1999). The Social origins of world hegemonies. In G. Arrighi & B. Silver (Eds.), *Chaos and governance in the modern world system* (pp. 151–216). University of Minnesota Press.

Simon, S. (2012, October 02). Privatizing public schools: Big firms eyeing profit from U.S. K-12 market. *Reuters*. Retrieved from: www.huntingtonpost.com

Stracqualursi, V. (2018). Kentucky governor says teachers' strike left children vulnerable to sexual assault. *CNN*. Retrieved from, www.cnn.com

Strassfeld, N., & Strassfeld, R. (2020). After Janus: Teachers' unions, walkouts, and social justice unionism. *International Journal of Education Reform, 29*(4), 334–353.

Strober, M., & Tyack, D. (1980). Why do women teach and men manage? A report on research in school. *Signs, 5*(3), 494–503.

Superville, D. (2016, November 15). Few women run the nation's school districts. Why? *Education Week*. Retrieved from, www.edweek.org

Swales, S. et al. (2020). Neoliberalism, guilt, shame and stigma: A Lacanian discourse analysis of food insecurity. *Journal of Community and Applied Social Psychology, 30*(6):673–687.

Tarrow, S. G. (2011). *Power in movement: Social movements and contentious politics*. Cambridge University Press.

Thomas, S. (2011). Teachers and public engagement: An argument for rethinking teacher professionalism to challenge deficit discourses in the public sphere. *Discourse: Studies in the Cultural Politics of Education, 32*(3), 371–382.

Tillman, L., & Trier, J. (2007). Boston Public as public pedagogy: Implications for teacher preparation and school leadership. *Peabody Journal of Education, 82*(1), 121–149.

Tosel, A. (2017). Hegemony as pedagogy: The formation of a collective will and of individual personality according to Gramsci. In N. Pizzolato & J. D. Holst (Eds.), *Antonio Gramsci: A Pedagogy to Change the World* (pp. 173–184). Springer.

Tuchman, G. (1978). *Making news*. Free Press.

Tufecki, Z. (2017). *Twitter and tear gas: The power and fragility of networked protest*. Yale University Press.

Uetricht, M. (2014). *Strike for America*. Verso.

Vaughn-Roberson, C. (1992). Having a purpose in life: Western women teachers in the twentieth century. In R. J. Altenbaugh (Ed.), *The Teachers's Voice, A social history of teaching in twentieth century America* (pp. 12–24).

Vogel, L. (1983/2013). *Marxism and the oppression of women: Toward a unitary theory* (Rev. ed.). Haymarket Books.

Waldman, P. (2018, April 2). Teachers are walking out in multiple states. Blame GOP economics. *The Washington Post*. Retrieved from, https://www.washingtonpost.com

Walgrave, S., & Van Aelst, P. (2006). The contingency of the mass media's political agenda setting power: Toward a preliminary theory. *Journal of Communication, 56*(1), 88–109.

Wallerstein, I. (2011). Dynamics of (unresolved) global crisis. In C. Calhoun & G. Derluguian (Eds.), *Business as usual: The Roots of the global financial meltdown*. NYU Press.

Weber, R. (2002). Extracting value from the city: Neoliberalism and urban redevelopment. In N. Brenner & N. Theodore (Eds.), *Spaces of neoliberalism: Urban restructuring in North America and Western Europe* (pp. 172–193). Blackwell.

Weber, R. (2010). Selling city futures: The financialization of urban redevelopment policy. *Economic Geography, 86*(3), 251–274.

Weber, R., & O'Neill-Kohl, S. (2013). The Historical roots of tax increment financing, or how real estate consultants kept urban renewal alive. *Economic Development Quarterly, 27*(3), 193–207.

Weiner, L. (2012). *The future of our schools: Teachers unions and social justice*. Haymarket Books.

Wright, E. O. (1980). Class and occupation. *Theory and Society, 9*(1), 177–214.

Wolfson, T. (2014). *Digital rebellion: The birth of the cyber left*. University of Illinois Press.

Zuboff, S., & Schwandt, K. (2019). *The age of surveillance capitalism: The fight for a human future at the new frontier of power*.

Zuckerman, E. (2013). Cute Cats to the Rescue? Participatory Media and Political Expression. In D. Allen & J. Light (Eds.), *Youth, New Media and Political Parties*. MIT Press.

Index

A
Althusser, Louis, 29, 58, 79, 80
American Federation of Teachers, 22, 65
American hegemony, 90
A Nation at Risk (Reagan administration education report), 7, 47, 77, 83, 85, 90
anti-Vietnam War movement, 20
Apple, Michael, 9, 10, 43, 56–58, 62, 64, 68, 72, 73, 75–77, 80, 82, 87–89, 92, 93, 123, 133
Arab Spring, 5, 8, 13, 18
Arizona teachers' strike, 3, 33, 34, 36, 37, 98, 99, 103, 110, 115, 128
Autonomist Marxism, 62
autonomy of teachers, 6, 7, 18, 43, 57, 58, 64, 65, 68, 80, 81, 144

B
banking model, 11, 29, 50
Bell, Terrel, 7
Bennett, L., 38, 117
Berliner, D., 9, 72, 85, 88

Bevin, Matt, 2, 131
Biddle, B., 9, 72, 85, 88
Black Lives Matter, 5, 13, 18
Bowles, S., 58, 75, 86
Bush administration
  Iraq War policy, 20
business unionism, 30–32, 35, 98

C
Caucus of Rank-and-File Educators. *See* CORE
centrality of education as a cultural arena, 75
centrality of education as a cultural institution, 14, 26
Chadwick, Andrew, 25
charter schools, 3, 4, 7, 10, 32, 34, 35, 49, 51, 77, 89, 91, 123, 126, 129, 131
Chicago, 10, 13, 22, 25, 30, 32, 33, 36, 37, 47–49, 65, 72, 77, 91, 120, 121, 126–128, 130, 132, 134

as a microcosm of the broader struggle, 32
as central location in teacher struggle, 10, 32
deindustrialization and white flight, 47
history of American Federation of Teachers, 65
importance of community organizing in the city, 25, 30, 33, 36, 37
laboratory for neoliberal education reforms, 49
laboratory of neoliberal education reforms, 72
neoliberal economic planning in the city, 48
Strikes in 2012, 2019, 3
Chicago Teachers' Federation, 65
2012 Chicago teachers' strike, 120, 127, 134
media portrayals of, 130
2019 Chicago teachers' strike, 130
Chicago Teachers' Union. *See* CTU
choice schools, 7, 32
circulation of discourses about education, 73
class position of teachers, 56–58
commercial news media, 120
community organizing by teachers, 3, 4, 7, 9, 10, 13, 14, 18, 25, 27, 29–36, 38, 39, 42, 48, 49, 63, 73, 74, 78, 80, 91–93, 109, 127
community organizing of teachers' unions, 73
CORE, 3, 4, 13, 22, 30, 32–35, 77, 90, 91
crisis in education, 124
crisis in education (as rhetoric justifying neoliberal reforms), 12
crisis of education, 88
crowds as an expression of public sentiment, 18, 24, 25, 27, 117
CTU, 3, 4, 7, 10, 12, 13, 25, 30, 32, 34, 72, 77, 78, 91, 121, 124, 125, 127, 130, 132–134

D
Daley, Richard, 47, 48
desegregation, 67
Deweyan view of the role of education in society, 80
Discussion and Information on social media, 115

E
education in crisis narrative, 74, 125
Emanuel, Rahm, 124, 126, 132, 134
ephemerality of digitally-enabled movements, 13, 19, 22, 26, 39, 117
episodic vs. thematic framing of education issues, 85
Every Student Succeed Acts, 50

F
Facebook, 13, 20, 21, 26, 36–39, 98–101, 103, 105, 106, 114–117
as networking tool for activists, 36
as organizing tool for activists, 37
use by teachers in the 2018 uprising, 98
Fordist mode of capitalist development, 42, 43, 45
Friere, Paolo, 11

G
gendered division of labor, 52, 60, 61, 64, 68
Gintis, H., 58, 75, 86

Global Social Justice Movement, 13
Google, 21, 36
Gramsci, Antonio, 10, 58, 79
Grassroots Education Movement, 30, 91

H
Haley, Margaret, 65, 66
Hall, Stuart, 78–80, 89, 122
  On there being no necessary correspondance between class position and ideology, 89
Hardt, M. and Negri, A., 21, 45
  notion of multitude, 21
hegemonic logics, 42
Herman and Chomsky's propaganda model, 79, 120
Hollywood portrayals of teachers 50s through to the 1990s, 83
horizontality as movement ideology, 20, 22
"hybrid media system", 25
hybrid movement (model for how the teachers' movement is organized), 25

I
ideological state apparatus, 79
immaterial labor, 45, 46, 57, 61, 62, 68, 69
Indignados, 5, 18
Indymedia, 20, 21, 26
International Monetary Fund, 51

J
Janus vs. AFSCME, 31
Johnson, Brandon, 4
Justice, Jim, 3

K
Kentucky Education Association, 2, 35
Kentucky teachers' strike, 2, 3, 35, 98, 131, 132

L
lean production, 43
Lewis, Karen, 10, 78, 91, 124, 132, 134

M
Marxist feminist tradition
  understanding of gendered labor, 60
Marx, K., 61
Mobilization using social media, 97, 106
Motivation of supporters using social media, 109, 113
movements of the squares, 5, 7, 8, 13, 18, 19, 22, 26, 116, 117

N
Narration of Cause using social media, 103
National Education Association, 22, 65
negative freedom, 45
neoliberalism
  as a disciplinary logic, 56
  as a dominant ideology, 121
  as an economic logic, 46
  as an ideology, 9
  as a pedagogical form, 10
  inequality and precariousness thereof, 117
  the subjectivity of, 87
networked counter-publics, 31
news media framing of teachers, 9, 72

No Child Left Behind, 11, 49
North American Free Trade Agreement, 19

O
Obama administration, 11, 50, 126
Occupy movement, 5, 8, 13, 18, 24, 26, 38
Oklahoma teachers' movement, 3, 22, 34, 37, 98, 99, 103, 108, 115, 130
Oklahoma Teachers' United, 22

P
Piketty, Thomas, 89
pop culture trope about inept teachers, 83
pop culture trope of inept teachers, 72
popular discourse on education policy, 81
productive and reproductive work, 60

R
Race to the Top, 11, 49, 50
#redfored, 33
red state rebellion, 34
Renaissance 2010, 49
Repertoire of Contention, 36
right to work laws, 30, 31, 37
role of education in society, 14, 26, 74, 80, 134, 135

S
savage inequalities frame of education coverage, 122, 125, 129, 132
Segerberg, A., 38, 117
signifying power, 135
The Simpsons portrayal of teachers, 84

Social media (as a tool of movement organization), 20, 26
social movement unionism, 13, 19, 29, 31, 32, 91, 98
Standard Aptitude Test, 49, 51
standardized test results, 7, 29, 56, 78
Strict Father Frame of education coverage, 122
subjectivity
 Marxist concept, 43

T
Tax Increment Financing, 47, 48
Taylorist mechanisms of control, 46, 64, 66
Teacher vs. the People Frame of education coverage, 122
techno-utopianism, 20
thematic vs. episodic framing of education issues, 74

V
Victorian cult of domesticity, 63, 65
Vogel, Lise, 59–61
voucher schools, 7

W
Wallerstein, Immanuel, 45
West Virginia teacher protests (2018), 2, 3, 34, 98, 103, 111, 112
World Economic Forum, 20
World Trade Organization protests in Seattle, 1999, 19

Z
Zapatistas, 19
Zuboff, Shoshana (Surveillance Capitalism), 20, 28, 36

GPSR Compliance

The European Union's (EU) General Product Safety Regulation (GPSR) is a set of rules that requires consumer products to be safe and our obligations to ensure this.

If you have any concerns about our products, you can contact us on ProductSafety@springernature.com

In case Publisher is established outside the EU, the EU authorized representative is:

Springer Nature Customer Service Center GmbH
Europaplatz 3
69115 Heidelberg, Germany

Batch number: 08679378

Printed by Printforce, the Netherlands